LISTENING
for the
HEARTBEAT OF GOD

LISTENING
for the
HEARTBEAT OF GOD

—— A Celtic Spirituality——

J. Philip Newell

PAULIST PRESS
New York / Mahwah, N.J.

Cover design by Cindy Dunne

First published 1997 by SPCK, Holy Trinity Church, Marylebone Road, London NW1 4DU. American edition published by Paulist Press copyright © J. Philip Newell 1997. Published by arrangement with SPCK, London.

Library of Congress Cataloging-in-Publication Data

Newell, J. Philip.
Listening for the heartbeat of God : a Celtic spirituality /
by J. Philip Newell.
p. cm.
Includes bibliographical references.
ISBN 0-8091-3759-3 (alk. paper)
1. Spirituality—Catholic Church. 2. Celtic Church—Doctrines.
3. Celts—Religion. 4. Peter, the Apostle, Saint.
5. John, the Apostle, Saint. I. Title.

BR748.N49   1997
270′.089′916—dc21
97-20783
CIP

Published by Paulist Press
997 Macarthur Boulevard
Mahwah, New Jersey 07430

www.paulistpress.com

Printed and bound in the
United States of America

To Ali

Contents

Preface

The gestation period for this book has been a long one. It was primarily during my time as Warden of Iona Abbey that I was awakened to the great treasury of Celtic spirituality. Living on this little holy island in the Hebrides which, as an Irish priest friend of mine once said, has about it 'something of the freshness of the first day of creation', I was well situated to receive the richness of Celtic spirituality's way of seeing, but it has been mainly over the intervening years that I have reflected and worked on this book, asking the question, 'How does a spirituality that is so creation-focused relate to life in the city and the way most of us live today?'

Because my reflection has not been in isolation but often in the context of lectures and retreats among people searching for ways of holding together their spirituality and their love of creation, my thanks are offered to the many on both sides of the Atlantic with whom I have explored these matters. Special thanks are due to certain individuals, however. In Scotland I think of Roland Walls of the Community of the Trans-figuration, who was the first to introduce me to the contemplative tradition's love of St John as the one who 'listened for the heartbeat of God', and of Noel

O'Donoghue, an Irish Carmelite, who, in addition to his writings in this field, very naturally exudes many of the characteristics of Celtic spirituality he breathed in as a boy in the hills of Killarney. I also thank Alec Cheyne, my Professor in Edinburgh, who guided me to the Celtic imagination of George MacDonald and related writings; Gilleasbuig Macmillan of St Giles' Cathedral, whose scepticism about the tendency to romanticize Celtic spirituality was insufficient to put me off seeing him as a representative of much of what is best in this stream of spirituality, and George MacLeod, the founder of the Iona Community, who was, in his prayers and in so many other ways as well, a great inspiration to me.

In North America too there are particular people whom I would like to thank. Cynthia Hirni and Robert Raines, formerly of the Kirkridge Retreat in Pennsylvania, encouraged me, in their delightfully affirming way, to believe that I should write this book. The many who have attended our annual talks at Kirkridge have further confirmed in me the sense of how widespread is the desire to reclaim such a spirituality. Looking much further back, I would like to thank my professor of English literature in Canada, Douglas Duncan, who, although he is not presumptuous enough to call himself a Celtic Christian, was in his spirit an important influence. His gift to me of a copy of the *Carmina Gadelica* was a timely one.

It is no reflection on England that my list here is much briefer, for I have been in this country for only a short time. There has in fact been a tremendous appetite within the Diocese of Portsmouth to receive from the Celtic stream of spirituality, and the invitation to do a series of lectures at the Cathedral provided me with the occasion to write the book essentially as it now stands.

Finally, the person who has worked most closely with me on this over the years is Alison, my wife. My deepest thanks are to her, despite the fact that when we have presented this type of material together she has sometimes been treated as a Celtic goddess and I as the mere carrier of her harp.

J. Philip Newell

Introduction

In the year 664, in a mixed religious community under the leadership of a woman, a Synod of the Church Catholic met to take a decision that was to alter the complexion of Christianity in Britain and perhaps much of the Western world. It was the Synod of Whitby and the abbess was Hilda. The monastery was a Celtic religious settlement of men and women in Northumbria, and in attendance were representatives of two missions, the Celtic and the Roman. The former had come through Aidan of Lindisfarne and before that from Iona and deferred to the authority of St John. The other had come through Augustine of Canterbury and before that from Rome and recognized the pre-eminence of St Peter. It is a tragedy that a decision was taken in favour of only one of these missions, so that the spirituality of the other began to be displaced.

The synod had been convened by Oswy, King of Northumbria, in whose kingdom the missions had clashed. There were differences of form and style, but essentially the conflict was between two spiritual perspectives or ways of seeing. The Celtic mission, inspired by John, remembered him as the beloved disciple who leaned against Jesus at the Last Supper. He had become an image of the practice of listening for the heartbeat of God. This spirituality lent itself to listening for God at the heart of life. The Roman mission, on the other hand, argued for the authority of Peter as the rock on which Christ had promised to build his Church. He had become a symbol of faithful action and outward unity. This spirituality favoured a listening for God in the ordained teaching and life of the Church. Oswy decided in favour of the Roman mission, which became the authorized religion of the land, while the Celtic mission began its formal decline.

Why was it that the two missions had come to have such distinct emphases? In particular, what had influenced and shaped the spirituality of the Celtic mission and its passion for finding God at the heart of all life? Where in its exile was the Celtic vision to find the space and acceptance to continue over the centuries, and what is its contribution today to those who are seeking a spirituality that is open both to listening for God in creation and in all people and to hearing God's word specifically in the Church? These are some of the issues to be explored in this book.

Celtic spirituality has come to mean different things to different people. For some it refers primarily to the spirituality of the ancient Celtic Church, especially as it developed before Whitby. For others it is identified largely with a New Age type of spirituality that, in seeking simplicity and freedom from institutional religion, has borrowed aspects of the old Celtic tradition. The premise of this book is that Celtic spirituality is neither simply a thing of the past nor a twentieth-century phenomenon. Rather, it is a spirituality that characterized the young British Church from as early as the fourth century. Although it was pushed out to the Celtic fringes of Britain after Augustine of Canterbury's

Roman mission in 597, it has always managed to survive in one form or another, usually on the edges of formal religion. This book sets out to trace the Celtic stream from the earliest centuries through the Synod of Whitby to today and to show that it is a spirituality of deep and rich perspective, with origins in the mystical traditions of the Old and New Testaments.

The feature of Celtic spirituality that is probably most widely recognized, both within and outside the Church, is its creation emphasis. It was certainly this that first drew my attention. Like most children, I had grown up with a sense of awe at creation. Our earliest memories are generally of wonder in relation to the elements. Do we not all carry within us, for instance, something of the memory of first listening to the waters of a river or to rainfall, or lying in the grass, feeling and smelling it and seeing its brilliant green, or watching sunlight dappling through leaves? Connected to these moments will be recollections of experiencing at the deepest of levels a type of communion with God in nature, but there will usually have been very little in our religious traditions to encourage us to do much more than simply thank God for creation. The preconception behind this is that God is separate from creation. How many of us were taught actually to look for God within creation and to recognize the world as the place of revelation and the whole of life as sacramental? Were we not for the most part led to think that spirituality is about looking away from life, so that the Church is distanced from the world and spirit is almost entirely divorced from the matter of our bodies, our lives and the world?

It was with a sense of liberation, therefore, that as a student I first read some of the old prayers from the

Western Isles of Scotland. In these the lights of the skies, the sun and moon and stars, are referred to as graces, the spiritual coming through the physical, and God is seen as the Life within all life and not just as the Creator who set life in motion from afar. It was particularly during my time at the Abbey on Iona, where many of these prayers had been forged and developed, that I became further convinced that this tradition of prayer is an important resource for the whole Church, for it makes the connection that is so often lacking between spirituality and the whole of life. Here, then, within the treasury of Christianity itself, was a rich stream of prayer that gave expression to something like the creation awareness that is being awakened among all sorts of people throughout the world today. And so I came to see that the prayers in the old Celtic tradition could aid our search for a spirituality that seeks God by looking towards the heart of life, not away from life.

The more familiar I became with these old prayers that had been passed down for centuries in the oral tradition, the more I began to ask myself, 'Where did this way of seeing come from, and where is it to be found today?' Asking these questions on Iona, it was relatively easy to begin to trace something of its course over the centuries. In the twentieth century, for example, I knew that George MacLeod, the founder of the Iona Community, had been influenced by the *Carmina Gadelica* tradition. Even the rhythm and images of his language in prayer recall the old prayers of the Hebrides. His way of seeing developed in new directions, social and political as well as ecological, the conviction that God is the Life of the world and not merely some religious aspect of it. To listen to God is to listen deep within ourselves, including deep within the collective life and consciousness of the world. Similarly, I was aware that in the nineteenth century, in the teachings of the Scottish 'heretic' Alexander Scott and in the writings of George MacDonald, the novelist, the characteristics of this tradition were to be seen, particularly the emphasis on the image of God at the heart of all people (as opposed to just the baptized or the chosen). Such thinking frightened religious orthodoxy because it challenged its boundaries, and so it was pushed to the very edge of the Church, where the Celtic tradition had time and again been forced to remain.

However, there still remained the question of where this distinct stream of spirituality had its source. Alexander Carmichael, who in the nineteenth century made the great collection of prayers from the Western Isles called the *Carmina Gadelica*, believed that many of them could ultimately be traced back to the Columban monastic community of Iona from the sixth century.

The prayers of the Western Isles and elsewhere in the Celtic world certainly reflect the same emphasis on creation as those attributed to St Columba and St Patrick, for instance. They continually portray the elements of the earth as expressions of God's grace and goodness and see God in the ordinary and everyday instead of exclusively in the Church.

I had discovered characteristics of the old Celtic Church in the prayers of the Western Isles, but where was the original source of this spiritual tradition? When I explored the earliest manifestations of Celtic Christianity, in the fourth-century writings of Pelagius, for example, I found a similar emphasis on the life of God within creation. This much-maligned early British Christian stressed not only the essential goodness of creation – and our capacity to glimpse what he called 'the shafts of divine light' that penetrate the thin veil dividing heaven and earth – but, very specifically, the essential goodness of humanity. Pelagius maintained that the image of God can be seen in every newborn child and that, although obscured by sin, it exists at the heart of every person, waiting to be released through the grace of God. He argued this despite increasing acceptance throughout the Western Church of Augustine's teaching that every child is born sinful. Augustine believed that the image of God can be restored to us only through the Church and its sacraments. He thus developed a spirituality that accentuated a division between the Church, which was seen as holy, on the one hand and the life of the world, perceived as godless, on the other.

It was the Celtic Church's emphasis on the presence of God at the heart of all life and within all people that prepared the ground for a clash with Augustine of Canterbury's Roman mission in 597, and it was this discord that eventually led to the Synod of Whitby's decision against the Celtic mission. Although formally rejected by the Church at large, the stream of Celtic spirituality survived. In the following centuries, especially in the art of the Celtic world, the same vision would be expressed in new and imaginative ways. The great high-standing crosses and the illuminated Gospel manuscripts incorporated designs that symbolized the interlacing of God and humanity, heaven and earth, spirit and matter. Similarly, in the ninth century the Celtic world produced one of its greatest theologians: John Scotus Eriugena, who taught that we can look to creation just as we look to the Scriptures to receive the living Word of God.

These were some of the people who preceded and influenced the Western Isles tradition of prayer that first drew my attention to Celtic spirituality. It is they, in addition to several key figures who followed and further developed it in the nineteenth and twentieth centuries, who form the subject matter of this book. A selective review of the history of Celtic spirituality is valuable in itself, providing as it does some continuity of perspective; it also demonstrates that this spirituality has been tried and tested over time. The main purpose of this book, however, is to offer what I believe to be a vital spirituality for today.

The most significant concept to emerge at the Synod of Whitby in 664 was the Celtic mission's perception of John as listening for the heartbeat of God. It revealed that this tradition did not begin with the Celtic Church and people like Pelagius, but was part of an ancient stream of contemplative spirituality stretching back to St John the Evangelist and even to the Wisdom tradition of the Old Testament. It was a spirituality characterized by a listening within all things for the life of God.

1 ✤ Listening for the Goodness: *Pelagius*

—⟳—

There are signs that Christianity arrived in Britain as early as the beginning of the third century. St Alban's martyrdom, for instance, occurred around 209. However, it is not clear what particular characteristics distinguished the spirituality of the early Church in Britain over its first few hundred years. The beginnings of the Church seem to have been linked to the Roman occupation and it is likely that the faith first came to Britain with the Roman army. The native population was still primarily tribal and rural. The imperial presence created an urban network and the early British Church took root in the towns within the orbit of the Roman army rather than spreading throughout the wider population in the countryside.

Not until the early fourth century did anything approaching a distinct British spirituality emerge. Its first prominent theologian was the Celtic Christian, Pelagius, whose teachings and spirituality have been seriously misrepresented over the centuries. Generations of theology students have been told about the dangerous heresy of Pelagius and the derogatory term 'pelagianism' has come to mean any doctrine that gives central place not to the redemptive grace of God but to our capacity to save ourselves. Seminarians have been instructed to write essays comparing Pelagius and Augustine, with no doubt as to who was to be the hero and who the villain. They have been told that virtually none of Pelagius' original writings remain, so that most of the source material about him – largely negative, at times even vitriolic – is by Augustine of Hippo. In fact, it now appears that much of Pelagius' work is available, although much of it has yet to be translated from the original Latin.

Who was this Celt who challenged one of the greatest fathers of the Church at an extremely sensitive point, generating torrents of criticism and centuries of misunderstanding? Pelagius, born in the latter half of the fourth century, was a Celtic Briton. Tradition has it that he was the son of a Welsh bard, which would help to explain his breadth of learning. He was a big, enthusiastic man; even his physical appearance became subject to adverse comment. St Jerome, for instance, speaks of him as slow – 'walking at the pace of a turtle' – and stupid from eating too much Scots porridge. Augustine's friend Orosius describes him as a huge, proud Goliath, over-confident in his own strength, and even criticizes Pelagius' hair-style, which may well have been an early example of the Celtic monastic style modelled on the pre-Christian Druidic tonsure (long but shaved around the sides and back), as opposed to the traditional Roman cut (shaved at the crown of the head). This same issue was to draw attention a few centuries later, at the Synod of Whitby, and of course was much more than a mere disagreement about hair-style. It signalled an unease about the Celtic mission's readiness to incorporate aspects of the thought and symbolism of the nature mysticism and religious

practice that preceded Christianity in Celtic Britain.
Early in the 380s Pelagius had travelled to Rome.
His presence was noticed and his style was different
and probably threatening to some, but it seems that he
was also regarded by many as a man of great personal
sanctity, of conviction and charisma. Initially he was
spoken of highly even by Augustine. In Rome he lived
as a lay monk, a common enough occurrence in the
early centuries and especially in the Celtic tradition.
He became known as a teacher and writer, as well as
a spiritual guide to some of the leading aristocratic
families of the Church in Rome. He apparently gathered a considerable following and his writings were
widely circulated.

These early writings of Pelagius contain themes that
would develop into some of the main characteristics
of the Celtic tradition over the following centuries.
Pelagius even makes reference, for example, to the
practice of finding an *anamchara* or 'soul friend', a well-
known feature of the spiritual discipline within the
Celtic Church in later centuries. Typically, he focuses
less on looking to the organized Church for spiritual
counsel than on finding in life a 'friend of the soul', one
to whom the inner self can be opened, 'hiding nothing', as Pelagius says, 'revealing everything' in order to
know and further explore what is in one's own heart.[1]

The most typical mark of the spirituality of the
Celtic tradition apparent in Pelagius' writings is his
strong sense of the goodness of creation, in which the
life of God can be glimpsed. Everywhere, he says, 'narrow shafts of divine light pierce the veil that separates
heaven from earth'.[2] To a friend he wrote:

> Look at the animals roaming the forest: God's
> spirit dwells within them. Look at the birds flying

across the sky: God's spirit dwells within them. Look at the tiny insects crawling in the grass: God's spirit dwells within them. Look at the fish in the river and sea: God's spirit dwells within them. There is no creature on earth in whom God is absent. . . . When God pronounced that his creation was good, it was not only that his hand had fashioned every creature; it was that his breath had brought every creature to life. Look too at the great trees of the forest; look at the wild flowers and the grass in the fields; look even at your crops. God's spirit is present within all plants as well. The presence of God's spirit in all living things is what makes them beautiful; and if we look with God's eyes, nothing on the earth is ugly.[3]

Because Pelagius saw God as present within all that has life, he understood Jesus' command to love our neighbour as ourself to mean loving not only our human neighbour but all the life forms that surround us. 'So when our love is directed towards an animal or even a tree,' he wrote, 'we are participating in the fullness of God's love.'[4]

Much of Pelagius' teaching can be seen to stem from the Wisdom tradition of the Old Testament. He saw Christ as the fulfilment of that tradition, as the perfect exemplar of wisdom and humility. Again, his Celtic emphasis was not so much on religious belief and the doctrines of the Church as on living a life of wisdom; by that he meant such things as loving all people, friends and enemies alike, and doing good in return for evil. He wrote to a new Christian:

You will realize that doctrines are inventions of the human mind, as it tries to penetrate the mystery

11

of God. You will realize that Scripture itself is the work of human minds, recording the example and teaching of Jesus. Thus it is not what you believe that matters; it is how you respond with your heart and your actions. It is not believing in Christ that matters; it is becoming like him.[5]

Although Pelagius was often accused of teaching that we can perfectly achieve the imitation of Christ, in his letters he frequently remarks how hard it is to follow Jesus and reveals how he personally is still falling far short of Jesus' simple precepts.

However, the fact that we repeatedly fail to follow the teachings of Jesus in our lives did not, for Pelagius, excuse us from setting Jesus' standard as our goal for living. He was very critical of those who tried to make a distinction between major offences and minor offences, for instance, so that refraining from murder or theft gives us licence to be less concerned about speaking harsh and hurtful words to one another, for example. Similarly, restraining ourselves from wrong deeds is of only relative value if we do not also do good deeds. 'A person who is rich,' he said, 'and yet refuses to give food to the hungry may cause far more deaths than even the cruellest murderer.'[6]

Specific reference is not made in the later condemnations of Pelagius to his passion for justice (a concern that led him even to call for the redistribution of wealth). Nevertheless, one wonders how far he had lost the support of the Church's leadership in Rome, where bishops and other ecclesiastical dignitaries had considerable wealth and power, now that Christianity was the established religion of the empire rather than that of a persecuted minority.

There are two areas in which explicit criticism of Pelagius does begin to emerge: his practice of teaching women to read Scripture and his conviction that in the newborn child the image of God is to be seen. These issues are clearly related, for the desire to educate women was rooted in Pelagius' conviction that God's image is to be found in every person, both male and female, and that the goodness of that image is nurtured and freed largely through the grace of wisdom. Jerome ✓ initiated the criticism by complaining that Pelagius was spending too much time talking and teaching indiscriminately in the public squares and crossroads, and especially that he was discussing the Scriptures with women, 'among their spindles and wickerwork', as he put it. He was unhappy, and perhaps even jealous, about the number of women attracted to Pelagius and particularly sarcastic about his belief that women should be taught to read and interpret the Scriptures. This may have seemed odd to Jerome and to the Roman world generally, but it is unlikely that Pelagius would have so regarded it: it was typical of his culture and would become the norm in the British Church. (As we shall see, the Celtic world was one that gave much greater ✓ scope to the role of women and more fully incorporated both the feminine and the masculine into its religious life and imagery. The Celtic mission integrated this aspect of their cultural inheritance into the Church's life and organization.) Pelagius' practice, then, rather than being seen as peculiar to him, can be regarded as reflecting the emerging attitudes of the Celtic Church.

The second, and much more controversial, feature of Pelagius' teaching to attract attention was his conviction that every child is conceived and born in the image of God. He believed that the newborn, freshly come forth from God, contains the original, unsullied goodness of creation and humanity's essential blessedness. This was in stark contrast to Augustine's thinking and the developing spirituality of the Church in the Roman world, which accentuated the evil in humanity and our essential unrighteousness. Augustine, with his sharp awareness of the pervasiveness of wrong-doing in the world, stated that the human child is born depraved and humanity's sinful nature has been sexually transmitted from one generation to the next, stretching from Adam to the present. Augustine believed that from conception and birth we lack the image of God until it is restored in the sacrament of baptism, and that con-ception involves us in the sinfulness of nature, sexual intercourse being associated with lustful desire. The perspective conveyed by Pelagius, on the other hand, is that to look into the face of a newborn is to look at the image of God; he maintained that creation is essentially good and that the sexual dimension of procreation is God-given. The emphasis that would increasingly be developed in the Celtic tradition was that in the birth of a child God is giving birth to his image on earth.

Pelagius' emphasis on the essential goodness of humanity did not involve a denial of the presence of evil and of its power over the human. Rather, it implied that at the heart of humanity is the image and goodness of God, a goodness that is obscured or covered over by the practice of wrongdoing and evil. Deeper than any wrong in us is the light of God, the light that no darkness has been able to overcome, as St John had written. At the heart of humanity is 'the light that enlightens every person coming into the world'. For Pelagius, evil was rather like an occupying army. The people yearn for liberation, but are bound by

14

forces of evil. Redemption, therefore, can be understood in terms of a setting free, a releasing of what we essentially are. Our goodness is sometimes so deeply buried as to be lost or erased, but it is there, having been planted by God, and awaits its release. For Pelagius, the redemption that Christ brings is such a liberation, a freeing of the good that is in us, indeed at the very heart of life.

Pelagius came under concentrated criticism from Augustine shortly after writing his public letter to a young woman named Demetrias, of a leading Roman family in Palestine. Demetrias, around the year 414, had sought the advice of Pelagius and others, including, it seems, Augustine, in relation to her vocation to a life of prayer. Early in the letter Pelagius further develops the theme that had been attracting attention, namely the essential innocence of a baby and the conviction that original sin is not present in the individual soul at conception. Adam's original sin, he believed, was to be seen strictly as an example of what happens when we do wrong, as opposed to being a debilitating fault that we inherit at conception. To Demetrias he wrote:

> First, then, you ought to measure the good of human nature by reference to its Creator. . . . If it is he who has made the world good, exceeding good, how much more excellent do you suppose that he has made humanity . . . fashioned in his own image and likeness. . . . Learn to appreciate the dignity of our human nature.[7]

Pelagius then invites Demetrias to 'approach the secret places of her soul' and there to be attentive to the 'inner teaching' that God has placed within her regarding her essential goodness and what she should do. Elsewhere

15

he had written that if we desire to find the light by which we are to live, we should look within our own hearts, for it is there that we will read the living Word of God. And if you seek a rule for your life, he says, 'write down with your own hand on paper what God has written with his hand on the human heart'.[8] Pelagius' conviction is that our deepest desires are for God and for what is good. There are of course other desires in us as well, confused and destructive ones, which can obscure the true self, but our deepest desires are good and come from God. That is why, says Pelagius, 'when a person gives generously to the poor and needy, and takes widows and orphans into his home, everyone knows that his actions are good and holy. People do not argue about whether generosity and forgiveness are good or bad; they know that they are good'.[9] Deep in their hearts, he goes on to say, they too want to be generous and forgiving. Conscience, and the inner capacity to know what is right and what is wrong, are rooted in the original righteousness of the soul, and the goodness of the image in which we are made has not been lost. This, he declares, has been 'implanted in all people', and this is what truly guides us to be what we have been created to be: the sons and daughters of God.

In his letter to Demetrias, Pelagius does not neglect to name the evil that is in and among us. 'We do not,' he says, 'defend the good of nature to such an extent that we claim that it cannot do evil; . . . we merely try to protect it from an unjust charge, so that we may not seem to be forced to do evil through a fault in our nature.'[10] Pelagius was concerned that Augustine's emphasis on human depravity leads to a loss of confidence in what we most essentially are, and to a downplaying

16

of the significance of the will in choosing to do either good or evil in our lives. This is not to deny the centrality of God's grace as the strength that enables us to choose and do what is right, but rather maintains that all is grace, our essential goodness of nature as well as our ability to choose the good and do it. What makes it difficult for us to do good, he contends in the letter, is the 'long habit of doing wrong which has infected us from childhood and corrupted us little by little over many years and ever after holds us in bondage and slavery to itself, so that it seems somehow to have acquired the force of nature'. Pelagius speaks of the habitual nature of sinning, and compares it to a person who drinks too much. At any moment such a person may choose to drink less, 'but the more he drinks the more he wants, and so the more difficult it becomes to restrain himself'.[11] He goes on to say that the more wrong is multiplied, the more our essential nature becomes buried and thus harder to recover, even to the point where we suppose, as Augustine did, that we have entirely lost it. Evil, he tells us, is like a fog that blinds us to our true selves.

One of the implications of Pelagius' emphasis is that it leads him to look for good and to expect to find it, well beyond the bounds of the Church. In relation to this he uses an analogy similar to the parable in Matthew 21 in which two sons are told to work in their father's vineyard; the son who says that he will work in fact does not, whereas the other gives no impression of intending to obey but does:

There are some who call themselves Christian, and who attend worship regularly, yet perform no Christian actions in their daily lives. There are others who do not call themselves Christian, and who never attend worship, yet perform many Christian actions in their daily lives. Which of these two groups are the better disciples of Christ? Some would say that believing in Christ and worshipping him is what matters for salvation. But this is not what Jesus himself said. His teaching was almost entirely concerned with action, and with the motives which inspire action. He affirmed goodness of behaviour in whoever he found, whether the person was Jew or Roman, male or female. And he condemned those who kept all the religious requirements, yet were greedy and cruel. Jesus does not invite people to become his disciples for his own benefit, but to teach and guide them in the ways of goodness. And if a person can walk along that way without ever knowing the earthly Jesus, then we may say that he is following the spirit of Christ in his heart.[12]

whoa

Pelagius asks Demetrias if we have not all met non-Christians who are good and kindly and just. 'From whence, I ask you, do these good qualities pleasing to God come, unless it be from the good of nature?'[13] Thus the grace of salvation received through the Church is given not to replace our nature but to release what is most fundamental in all people, although bound by the oppression of sin and wrongdoing. This indicates a relationship between the Church and the world very different from the Augustinian model. Rather than accentuating the distinctions between them, the ministry of the Church is to liberate and free the goodness of God that is already at the very heart of all life, yearning, as St Paul would say, for its release.

The Church becomes liberator rather than custodian ✓ of salvation. It provides the key that gives access to the treasure of God's life instead of being the source of that richness; the treasure is already present, though hidden, waiting to be unlocked, in every person.

Just as this treasury is discovered by some outside the Church, so it was opened by others before the birth of the Church. Pelagius cites Job, for instance, as 'a man of the gospel', describing him as a man who 'by opening up the hidden wealth of nature and bringing it out into the open, revealed by his own behaviour what all of us are capable of and has taught us how great is that treasure in the soul which we possess but fail to use, and, because we refuse to display it, believe that we do not possess it either.'[14] For Pelagius, the gift of the gospel is that we are 'instructed by the grace of Christ', encouraged and shown the goodness of God that is within us.[15] In his spiritual teachings, he advises that we should listen within ourselves and then compare what we hear with Jesus. 'If you have formulated principles which are contrary to his teaching,' he says, 'then you have misheard your conscience, and you must listen anew.'[16] If, on the other hand, what we hear conforms to Jesus' teaching, then we can be satisfied that we have heard correctly.

After the publication in Palestine of Pelagius' letter to Demetrias, Augustine sent his friend Orosius to Jerusalem with the intention of convicting Pelagius of heresy. Two attempts were made to condemn him in 415, but twice Pelagius was acquitted by the Church in Palestine. In 416 Augustine and the African bishops reacted by convening two diocesan councils, at which Pelagius and his Celtic friend Celestius were condemned. In the following year the Pope himself convened a synod in Rome to consider the conflict; here Pelagius' teaching was declared entirely true and orthodox. In an attempt to reconcile Pelagius' emphasis on our essential goodness with Augustine's emphasis on the prevalence of evil, the Pope wrote to the African bishops, 'Love peace, prize love, strive after harmony. For it is written: "Love your neighbour as yourself."' The Pope's guidance was not heeded by Augustine and the Western Church began to lose sight of the essential God-given goodness of the human. This loss would have implications for the Church's perspective on the world, as a fundamentally unholy realm.

The African bishops, frustrated by the Pope, now pursued the route of State intervention, securing the condemnation of Pelagius under an imperial edict dated 30 April 418. He was banished from Rome, essentially on a charge of disturbing the peace. With the Emperor's judgement against him, a Church condemnation followed within months. In the midsummer of 418 Pelagius was excommunicated, although on what formal grounds remains unclear. What is certain, however, is that the forces which moved against him that year were primarily political in nature.

After his banishment and excommunication it seems that Pelagius went back to Wales, possibly to the protection of a Welsh monastery (tradition associates him with Bangor). Whether or not Pelagius did return there, the important point to grasp is that many of the spiritual characteristics apparent in the Celtic Church in Britain at this time and during the next few hundred years are consistent with those of Pelagius' spirituality. In other words, Pelagius was not a one-off 'heretic', but, like his Celtic friend Celestius, reflected the emerging spirituality of the young Celtic Church in Britain. In the years immediately following Pelagius' excommuni-cation, and even over 200 years later, papal concern was expressed about 'Pelagian' theology in Britain, and, as the twentieth-century German theologian Karl Barth said – not intending to pay us a compliment – the British remain 'incurably Pelagian' to this day.

In all likelihood Pelagius, under both imperial ban and Church excommunication, did return to the sanc-tuary of the Celtic world. Ireland, having never been part of the Roman Empire, was particularly safe, and it is interesting that it is especially in fifth-century Irish manuscripts of Scripture exposition that references like 'Pl states' and 'Pl says' proliferate. In Celtic writings of the next number of centuries, and most markedly in those from Ireland, even until as late as the ninth century, references to Pelagius and his scriptural *Expositiones* are plentiful. One of the most delightful ironies surrounding his excommunication, when he was forced to write pseudonymously, is that he signed much of his work 'Augustine' or 'Jerome'; under these names his writings circulated throughout Europe for centuries.

It is valuable to examine the earliest features of Christian spirituality in Britain not simply because it teaches us about the past and helps us to decide whether history has dealt fairly with the first British theologian. More importantly, it enables us to explore our own spirituality today, and to consider whether our way of seeing has been impoverished by the loss of the perspective that existed in the early Celtic Church. If we believe that at birth we lack the image of God and are essentially sinful, what are the implications for our spirituality? Does it mean that there is no vital connection between true spirituality and the sort of purity, simplicity, innocence and goodness of an infant?

If we deny that God is at the very heart of life, are we essentially without God, without original goodness in our mothers' wombs, so that our spirituality does not grow out of what God has planted within us? Is spirituality alien to our original nature, or does grace nurture our innate goodness? What about our relationship with the rest of humanity? If we regard others as lacking essential goodness because they are outside the Church's sacramental ministry, does that mean that our spirituality has nothing to learn from other faiths and from the virtues that, as Pelagius reminds us, can be observed in our neighbours, many of whom are not members of the established Christian Church? For us, as for Pelagius and the young Celtic Church, these are important questions to ask.

It is not known how Pelagius responded personally to his excommunication or how it affected him spiritually. What is clear is that he had been certain in his own mind about how he wished to act in the face of persecution. 'Wisdom,' he wrote, 'consists in listening to the commandments of God, and obeying them. A person who has heard that God commands people to be generous, and then shares what he has with the poor, is truly wise.' He also said, 'a person who has heard that God commands people to forgive . . . and then reaches out in love to his persecutors, is truly wise'.[17] As we shall see, at nearly every stage in its development the Celtic tradition would need this sort of inner strength and resolve, because it would be beset by the opposition and misunderstanding of the wider Church.

2 ❖ Listening within Creation:
Eriugena

━━━∿∿RR̂R̂🅐R̂R̂∿∿━━━

Pelagius' ban and excommunication early in the fifth century occurred at almost exactly the same time as another event of great significance for Christianity in Britain: the barbarian invasions and the sack of Rome in the year 410. The latter resulted in the withdrawal from Britain of the Roman army, along with it the removal of the superstructure under which the young British Church had taken root. It was as if Pelagius and the Romans passed each other in the night, Pelagius returning to the Celtic world for sanctuary and the Romans heading back to the Mediterranean, while Angles and Saxons swept into Britain. Thus began an almost 200-year separation between the Celtic branch of the Church and any significant influence of the Church in Rome. It was during this period that Celtic spirituality developed and flourished, in a land free from Roman domination.

One of Pelagius' great contemporaries in the Celtic world was Ninian (*c.* 360–*c.* 432), who, having trained in Rome and come under the influence of St Martin of Tours in Gaul, returned to his native Cumbria and began the mission based at the monastic church of

Candida Casa in Whithorn. Ninian modelled his mission not on the Roman town and diocesan structure but on the Eastern monastic model more suited to the still essentially rural and tribal nature of the Celtic lands. Thus began a distinctively Celtic mission to the Picts and Britons of present-day Scotland. It consisted of clusters of monks living in community in rural Celtic settlements, the monasteries acting as centres of Christian life and prayer, as well as of education and mission.

Around the same time, *c.* 430, St Patrick, who was probably originally of the Ninianic Church, began his mission to Ireland. It is in the early Irish mission that we see a fuller emergence of some of the main distinguishing features of Celtic spirituality, including an awareness of the goodness of creation and a sense of the company of heaven's presence among us on earth. What comes across again and again in the prayers and art of the early Irish Church is this intertwining of the spiritual and the material, heaven and earth, time and eternity. Although the famous 'Breastplate' hymn attributed to St Patrick probably dates from a later period and was not actually written by him, its themes reflect the major characteristics of Celtic Christianity. In the third verse of the hymn the graces of the elements are invoked in a way that suggests that the spiritual exists within the matter of creation and that God's healing and restoring powers are to be found in the goodness of the earth. Just as Pelagius emphasized our essential God-given goodness, so in the tradition of St Patrick there is an awareness that all created things carry within them the grace and goodness of God. Thus the hymn, in invoking the strength of God, invokes the energies of the elements:

I bind unto myself today
The virtues of the star-lit heaven,
The glorious sun's life-giving ray,
The whiteness of the moon at even,
The flashing of the lightning free,
The whirling wind's tempestuous shocks,
The stable earth, the deep salt sea
Around the old eternal rocks.

These words of looking to God for strength and therefore looking to the elements of creation, leap out of our hymn-books. They make a profounder and more vital connection between the spiritual and the material than what we are accustomed to find in other hymns that merely touch upon the beauty of creation at a superficial level. They draw our attention not simply to the goodness of what has been created but to a perception that within creation there is something of the presence of the uncreated, that is, God. We need to ask what it is about an emphasis on the spiritual being within the material that has so often frightened Western traditions of spirituality, to the point that, although words like these are attributed to a saint of the Western Church, they are in fact omitted from versions of the hymn in many hymn-books and in others treated merely as optional.

The second characteristic, that of the closeness of heaven's company among us on earth, comes across especially in the sharply Christocentric fifth verse of St Patrick's hymn. Christ is everywhere present and with him the host of heaven:

Christ be with me, Christ within me,
Christ behind me, Christ before me,
Christ beside me, Christ to win me,

25

Christ to comfort and restore me,
Christ beneath me, Christ above me,
Christ in quiet, Christ in danger,
Christ in hearts of all that love me,
Christ in mouth of friend and stranger.

There is not in the Celtic way of seeing a great gap
between heaven and earth. Rather, the two are seen as
inseparably intertwined. Mary, for instance, loved with
a homely tenderness of affection, is portrayed not as
Queen of Heaven, remote from humanity, but as a
barefooted country girl out among the cattle, in immediate contact with the concerns and delights of daily
life. Peter is perceived not as an exalted ecclesiastic but
as a simple fisherman, experienced in the ways of the
sea, present to guide and to guard, and Christ, as King
of the Elements, is not regarded as a distant regal figure
but more in terms of the Celtic king, chief of the tribe,
known to his people and close to them. The Christ
who is above them in the brightness of the morning
sun is the Christ who is beneath them in the dark
fertility of the earth. The Christ who is with his people
in the quiet calm of a windless sea is with them too in
the midst of the wild wintry storm. The Christ who is
within, at the very centre of their soul, is the Christ
who is to be looked for in friend and stranger, Christ
at the heart of all life.

It was in the century following Patrick's mission to
Ireland that there came the greatest flourishing of
Celtic spirituality. An island that had been relatively
unaffected by the Roman presence and had remained
free from Anglo-Saxon invasion and cultural intrusion,
sixth-century Ireland witnessed a creative encounter
between the Christianity that Patrick and others had

brought and the nature mysticism of the pre-Christian Druidic religion. With the gospel had come a whole new world of literature and story, the hope of eternal life and a belief in spirit not confined to matter. In the years after the seed of the gospel was planted in Irish soil there came an extraordinary growth of imagination and cultural-religious activity among the people of Ireland. With the willingness of the early Irish Christians to accept rather than eliminate many aspects of the earlier religion, the pre-Christian nature mysticism became almost like the Old Testament of the Celtic Church.

When we look at a map of the Celtic lands even today we can see that their evangelization, begun in the fifth century, did not erase the marks of pre-Christian religion but rather transformed them, allowing some of the old stories and holy place-names and traditions to be woven into the fabric of the gospel tradition. A well that had been named after a Druidic goddess might be renamed St Mary's Well, while the neighbouring glen would continue to be called the Glen of the Fairies. There was no desire to change everything or to sweep away all that had gone before it; instead, the gospel was permitted to work its mystery of transformation in the life and culture of the people. The gospel was seen as fulfilling rather than destroying the old Celtic mythologies.

A sixth-century bard claimed that Christ had always been the Celts' teacher, but they had not known him by name. It was in a way a mission modelled on St Paul's sermon to the Athenians. Having discovered among them an altar dedicated to 'an unknown god', Paul had told the Athenians, 'What therefore you worship as unknown, this I proclaim to you . . .', proceeding to speak of the One in Whom 'we live and move and have our being' (Acts 17:16–34). The Celtic mission's proclamation of the gospel led to a knowledge of the Word that had always been in the people, a naming of the light that had always been theirs because it is the light that enlightens every person who comes into the world. The gospel was like a grace of self-revelation. It freed them to become more truly, rather than less truly, themselves..

Although there was some resistance to the conversion of Ireland to Christianity, there is not a single account of martyrdom in the Celtic mission. The readiness to accept the gospel and to bring to Christianity the riches of the Celtic religious heritage is conveyed in the legendary version of the Epiphany story that has come to be broadly accepted throughout the Church. The Druids' Latin name had been *Magi*, so the Celtic Church developed its Epiphany story in terms of three Magi bringing the gifts and the ancient wisdom of their people to the feet of Christ.

Stories of the sixth-century St Brigid provide examples of these features of the young Irish Church and its spirituality. It was said that Brigid's mother had been baptized by Patrick and that her father had been a Druid priest. In legend, therefore, she symbolized this meeting of the gospel with pre-Christian Ireland. Pre-Christian myths about the goddess Brigid were assimilated into the Celtic Church's stories about the sixth-century St Brigid, often with scant regard for historical congruity. In the Irish story of the Nativity, for example, Brigid is cast as the barmaid at the inn in Bethlehem where there was no room for Mary and Joseph to stay. Brigid is described as offering them a bannock and a drink, drawing on the inn's dwindling supply of oatmeal and water; at the birth of the Christ-child she becomes both midwife and wet-nurse. Thus in this legend the Christian gospel, newly arrived in Ireland, is symbolically portrayed as suckled at the breasts of the country's nature mysticism and mythology.

We do know that Brigid was the sixth-century Abbess of Kildare. Kildare means 'church of the oaks' and oak groves had of course been sacred places for the Druids. It is typical of the Celtic Church not to have destroyed or ignored the ancient oak groves but to have transformed them into centres of its mission. Kildare was a Celtic religious community for both men and women. There were many such double monasteries, for the Celtic Church neither totally separated the sexes nor displayed the fear of sexuality that was to dominate much of the Western Church. As in Eastern orthodoxy, there were married priests and celibate monks, but the ecclesiastic leadership of women such as Brigid was peculiar to the Celtic Church.

The Irish came to revere Brigid as their patron – or, rather, mother – saint, second only to Patrick. Many of the stories about these saints associate them with the belief in the intrinsic goodness of creation. Brigid is said to have used herbal remedies, a practice that points to their conviction that God's restorative graces were hidden in earth's elements.

Stories about sixth-century saints like Brendan and Columba, and their love of creation, abound. Prayers in the Columba tradition connect him to a spirituality that was intensely aware of the earth, sea and sky. Columba he writes of wanting to hear 'the thunder of the crowding waves upon the rocks' and to experience the roar of the surrounding sea and the rich light of the low sun over the Atlantic while at prayer on his holy island. The stories about Columba convey a commitment to Christ and at the same time a willingness to accept traditional Irish culture and religion as precursors to the gospel. Columba refers to Christ as 'my Druid', and it seems that the isand of Iona was, like Brigid's Kildare, a pre-Christian holy site transformed into a centre of Christian mission.

Even in the sixth century, but especially in the seventh, there was a great explosion of missionary activity from Iona and other Celtic monastic sites, not only to the Celtic peoples of Scotland but to the Angles and Saxons in England and as far east as Russia. Columbanus' mission to Europe occurred at this time, for instance. (Interestingly, he aroused opposition in Rome and elsewhere because his teachings were akin to those of Pelagius, and viewed as irregular and suspect, largely because they were Irish in origin.) It was in the seventh century also that Aidan began his mission from Iona to Northumbria and established the monastery of Lindisfarne.

As the Celtic mission moved further south in Britain, a mission from Rome re-established itself and began to move north. In the year 597 Augustine of Canterbury had begun his mission to Britain. The separation of the Celtic and Roman missions, which had lasted nearly 200 years, came to an end. In the intervening period there had been significant changes on both fronts. In the continental Church an increasing uniformity had developed throughout the empire in relation to religious practices including the dating of Easter. The Bishop of Rome, whose power and primacy had been further consolidated, was largely responsible for this policy. Augustine of Hippo's theological emphasis on human depravity had come into even greater prominence and celibacy laws for the priesthood had become the norm, widening the separation between male and female in the Church. In the Celtic mission, on the other hand, there was a growing emphasis on the goodness of creation, clergy were still permitted to marry, the distinction between religious and lay was not hard and fast, and women, although not ordained into the priesthood, held positions of leadership in the Church.

It is not surprising that the more these missions came into contact with each other, the more tension grew. In Northumbria, for instance, King Oswy had been baptized by the Celtic mission and his Queen Eanfleda by the mission from Rome. The ensuing domestic crisis at the Northumbrian court, where the king and queen celebrated Easter at different dates, reflected the tension that was becoming widespread.

Finally, in 664, a synod was convened at the double monastery of the Abbess Hilda in Whitby. At one level it might appear that the synod's discussions, about such matters as the dating of Easter and the style of tonsure to be worn, were superficial. The underlying debate was a very significant one, however, for at stake were the futures of two distinct types of spirituality which had come into conflict and were vying for supremacy. In his *Ecclesiastical History*, Bede describes how Bishop Coleman of Lindisfarne, arguing the case for the Celtic mission, appealed to the authority of St John, as the disciple who had leaned against Jesus at the Last Supper and heard the Lord's heartbeat. Abbot Wilfrid, on the other hand, presenting the case for the Roman mission from Canterbury, argued for the authority of St Peter, to whom Jesus had said: 'Thou art Peter, and upon this rock I will build my Church' (Matthew 17:18). After much debate King Oswy decided in favour of the Roman mission, saying, 'I shall not contradict Peter.'

The great tragedy of the Synod of Whitby is that neither the Peter tradition nor the John tradition should have been displaced. Each represents a way of seeing firmly rooted in the gospel tradition. The decision of the synod was a fundamental rejection of the perspective of the Celtic mission. The St John tradition, with its emphasis on the Light that enlightens every person coming into the world, had inspired the Celtic mission to believe, like Pelagius, in the essential goodness of humanity. Similarly, St John's vision of God as the Life of the world had led this mission to look for the grace of God within as well as beyond creation. The concept of listening for the heartbeat of God within all things, ourselves, one another and the whole of creation was a feature of the spirituality of the Celtic mission that now began to be displaced.

After the Synod of Whitby the Celtic mission entered into decline. Coleman's removal from Lindisfarne to Ireland represents the beginning of its retreat. The Roman mission now occupied Lindisfarne and replaced the small wooden structures of the Celtic monastery with a church built of stone, symbolizing its strength and organization, but also the sharper division between the place of worship and creation. In northern England, Wilfrid and the Roman mission began systematically to replace Celtic practices and monastic way of life with the Roman liturgy and Benedictine monasticism from the continent.

The decline of the Celtic mission did not occur overnight, of course, and in a sense some of its best contributions were still to come. In some places, such as Iona, it took centuries for the decree of Whitby to be implemented or obeyed, and the stream of Celtic spirituality would never entirely cease. Adamnan, Abbot of Iona, outwardly conformed to Oswy's ruling in 688, nearly 25 years after the Synod of Whitby, but when he returned to Iona with a Roman tonsure he was rejected by his monks. The Celtic monastery of Iona was a centre of resistance to the Roman mission for nearly 200 years, the last independent Abbot of Iona dying in the year 860.

This period of resistance on the Isle of Iona was marked by an artistic creativity that reflected the continuing vitality of the Celtic Church's spiritual life. Some of its most beautiful illuminated manuscripts of the Gospels were produced over these centuries; it is likely that the monks of Iona started working on the *Book of Kells*, for instance, around the year 800. The Celtic combination of the love of creation on the one hand and the love of Scripture on the other is expressed in the brilliantly coloured and superbly crafted illuminations of gospel text. Heaven and earth, the visible and the invisible, are depicted as intertwined, angel faces peeking out at the end of one strand of design, plants or animals or human faces appearing at the end of the next. Celtic art's 'everlasting pattern', as it has come to be known, was used to suggest the eternal interweaving of heaven and earth, time and eternity – the immediacy of God in all created life.

These illuminated Gospel manuscripts and the continuing themes of Celtic spirituality that they conveyed were echoed by the great high-standing crosses of the Celtic Church. In the St John's and St Martin's Crosses of Iona, for instance, dating from the eighth and ninth centuries respectively, creation and Scripture themes are again combined and inseparable. The orb at the centre of the cross, probably representing the sun and the light of the world, and certainly the Scripture and nature images carved on opposite sides of the cross, express the desire to hold together the revelation of God in creation and the revelation of God in the Bible. They reflect the practice of listening for the living Word of God in nature as well as in the Scriptures.

This was certainly the conviction of the ninth-century philosopher John Scotus Eriugena, perhaps the greatest teacher the Celtic branch of the Church ever produced. His name, a complicated one to the modern ear, simply means 'John the Irishman from Ireland'. Eriugena taught that Christ moves among us in two shoes, as it were, one shoe being that of creation, the other that of the Scriptures, and stressed the need to be as alert and attentive to Christ moving among us in creation as we are to the voice of Christ in the Scriptures.

Who was this man and what was his contribution to the development of Celtic spirituality? Eriugena was born in the early ninth century in Ireland, but by the middle of the century had travelled to France, where he became head of the court school of Charles the Bald (King of France and later Holy Roman Emperor). On other fronts the Celtic mission was in decline, but Eriugena took Celtic spirituality to the very heart of the Western Empire. Being neither a monk nor a priest, he was relatively free from ecclesiastical censure. Nevertheless, at times he was accused of reviving Pelagius' thought and, because of his emphasis on creation, of pantheism. At one point he was even subjected to the same sort of racial slur as Pelagius when his teachings were critically described as 'Scots porridge'. It was not until long after his death, however, that Eriugena's works were formally condemned by the Pope.

Like the Celtic Christian teachers before him, Eriugena's thought was particularly shaped by the mysticism of St John, whom he described as 'the observer of the inmost truth'. John, he said, had listened within and heard the Word through whom all things are made, the Word that is at the heart of life and from which all that is comes forth. If God were to stop speaking the whole created universe would cease to exist. In the rising of the morning sun God speaks to us of grace and new beginnings, and the fertility of the earth is a sign of how life wells up from within, from the dark unknown place of God. In his homilies on the prologue to St John's Gospel, Eriugena tells us that God is in all things, the essence of life; God has not created everything out of nothing, but out of his own essence, out of his very life. This is the light that is in all things, 'the light which is the light of angels, the light of the created universe, the light indeed of all visible and invisible existence'.[1] The world, therefore, Eriugena regarded as theophany, a visible manifestation of God. Even what seems to be without vital movement, like the great rocks of the earth around us, has within it the light of God. To know the Creator, we need only look at the things he has created. The way to learn about God, Eriugena believed, is 'through the letters of Scripture and through the species of creation'. He urges us to listen to these expressions of God and to 'conceive of their meaning in our souls'.

Like the writer to the Hebrews, Eriugena regarded all that is visible as having come forth from that which is invisible, all that is seen as issuing from what is unseen. The immaterial, he said, is the cause of the material; the life of God within is the source of all that is outward and physical. Because the essence of our life comes from

God and is rooted in God, Eriugena emphasized that we are to be aware of the unity and simplicity of God that underlies the multiplicity and complexity of outward life. The attitude of Eriugena and Celtic spirituality generally on this point is diametrically opposed to the sort of materialism we know in the Western world today. Matter is regarded as the essence of life and may or may not give rise to spiritual thought and expression. Eriugena's view on the other hand was that the spiritual is at the heart of life and that the more deeply we look into matter the closer we will come to God.

In his greatest work, *Periphyseon* (Division of Nature), Eriugena further developed Celtic spirituality's belief in the essential goodness of creation. God's divine goodness is, he wrote, 'the essence of the whole universe and its substance'.[2] So essentially good is creation that if the good were entirely abstracted from it, everything would cease to exist; nothing would remain. Putting this in philosophical terms, he said that goodness is not an attribute of being; rather being is an attribute of goodness. In other words, goodness is not simply a feature of life but gives rise to life. Evil, therefore, is opposed to existence; whereas goodness is creative, evil is destructive. Eriugena insisted that nothing in nature is evil in itself. That is, we and all creation bear within us, however covered over it may be, the essential goodness of God. If we become evil, we are acting contrary to our essential nature. Eriugena's spirituality led him not to look away from life but further within; he believed that when we look within ourselves, and within all that exists, we will find darknesses and evil but, deeper still, the goodness of God.

He regarded grace not as opposed to nature but as

co-operating with it, restoring it or releasing its essential goodness. He taught that what has been lost is not the light that is within all life, for, as St John says, the darkness has not overcome it. Rather, what has been lost, says Eriugena, is 'the true beholding of the light from the inner eyes'.[3] Grace is given to heal that inner sight, to open our eyes again to the goodness that is deep within us, for God is within us. The grace of Christ restores us to our original simplicity. Everything that is divided is reunited, whether the division is between heaven and earth, between the visible and invisible, or between male and female. With an emphasis that reflected the ancient Celtic Church's practice, almost entirely lacking elsewhere, Eriugena stressed that the unity at the heart of life in which we are to be restored is neither a male reality nor a female reality, for 'the image of God', he said, 'is neither male nor female.'[4] These distinctions appear only at the surface of life, not at its heart.

Eriugena's influence on the thought and spirituality of the ninth century was considerable. In addition to his own writings, he, through his scholarship and translating work, brought to the West some of the Eastern Church's ancient mystical insights. His translation of the *Celestial Hierarchy*, written by a fifth-century mystical theologian known as Dionysius the Pseudo-Areopagite, in which the realms of angels and other messengers of God's light are described, provided the basis for much of the Church's understanding of the angelic as mediating God to humanity and heaven to earth. This was a further manifestation of the Celtic Church's delight in the angelic and of its conviction that the ladder that connects heaven and earth, and on which the messengers of

God's glory are continually ascending and descending, is everywhere present.

Eriugena's thought and writings were increasingly suspected of pantheism, 'God being all things'. A more accurate term to describe them would be panentheism, 'God in all things'. In 1225 his main treatise was condemned by the Pope and in 1685 it was placed on the Index, the papal list of forbidden writings. Once more a significant contribution from the Celtic stream of spirituality was being rejected by the Church at large, but its seeds had been deeply sown. Eriugena's spirituality would find expression again in later mystics such as Meister Eckhart and Johann Tauler, for instance, and many who followed in this contemplative tradition in centuries to come.

3 ✤ Listening for God in All Things: *Carmina Gadelica*

While Eriugena was making his Celtic contribution to the thought and spirituality of the Holy Roman Empire, the last outward vestiges of the old Celtic Church in Britain were rapidly disappearing, with a few exceptions here and there, notably on the island of Iona. In Scotland a late conformity to the Roman mission was given its greatest boost by the marriage of Margaret to King Malcolm in 1061. St Margaret, of an English royal family, brought with her a passionate commitment to the uniformity of the Church Catholic and therefore a determination to bring into line the remaining pockets of opposition to conformity. The rebuilding in stone of St Oran's chapel on Iona, the greatest bastion of resistance to the Roman mission, speaks of the extent of her success, although, even after Queen Margaret, Culdee chapels were dotted around Scotland. The Culdees, Celtic monks in the eremitic tradition, had gradually banded together into loosely structured monastic clusters and can be regarded as the last tangible remnant of the old Celtic Church.

Probably the final sign of formal conversion to the Roman mission in Scotland was the building of the Benedictine monastery on Iona in the thirteenth century. The island's last Celtic monks were either expelled or absorbed. At this point the Celtic mission can be said ⅄ to have ceased to exist in any structured religious form. This is not to say, however, that its stream of spirituality came to an end. The Roman mission may have built the strong stone Benedictine Abbey on Iona, the site of the old Celtic mission, but the spirituality of the latter and its distinct way of seeing was to live on among the people of the Western Isles.

In the middle of the nineteenth century a civil servant from Edinburgh named Alexander Carmichael (1832–1912) began to record the prayers that had been passed down for centuries in the oral tradition of the Hebrides and the west coast of Scotland. For generation after generation, parents had been teaching their children prayers whose origin stretched back beyond living memory. These prayers, usually sung or chanted rather than simply said, were recited as a rhythmic accompaniment to the people's daily routine, at the rising of the sun and at its setting, at the kindling of the fire in the morning and at its covering at night. They were chanted individually while sowing the seed in the fields and collectively by women weaving cloth together. These prayers were used in the most ordinary contexts of daily life and not within the four walls of a church on Sunday, but Carmichael detected in many of them a liturgical character and tone. He believed they had come down in the tradition of the old Celtic Church, and the chanting that accompanied them was reminiscent of its ancient music.

Although the Celtic mission had been outwardly

suppressed, its tradition of prayer and spirituality lived on, almost like a spiritual resistance movement, among the people of the Western Isles and, as we shall see, its prayers were cherished and developed, often under the most adverse pressure and even persecution from the established churches. It is interesting to note (bearing in mind the Synod of Whitby and the Celtic mission's claim to the authority of John), that the references in these prayers to St John are with affection. He is called 'John of love' or 'John the Beloved', sometimes even 'foster-son of Mary' or 'foster-brother of Christ', foster-ship in the Highlands being regarded as one of the closest and most tender relationships.

The most striking characteristic of Celtic spirituality in these prayers is the celebration of the goodness of creation. It is not surprising that in the Western Isles there should have been a sharp awareness of the earth and sea and sky. The people's livelihood depended entirely on the elements. Carmichael describes how they spoke when they met on the paths or in one another's homes, sometimes for gatherings called 'ceilidhs' where the old stories, songs and prayers were heard again and again. Their conversations were often about the skies, the effects of the sun on the earth and the moon on the tides, or the ebbing of the sea and the life in its depths. In all of this, Christ was referred to as 'King of the elements', 'Son of the dawn' or 'Son of the light'.

The prayers in the Carmichael collection, known as the *Carmina Gadelica*, meaning simply 'the songs and poems of the Gaels', can seem romantic if we forget the harshness of the conditions under which they were forged and handed down. The sea was frequently dangerous and took the lives of many islanders, and much of the terrain was inhospitable. When crops failed there was terrible hardship and famine. Nevertheless, creation was regarded as essentially good. One of the prayers of blessing, for instance, reveals how, before a journey or a parting, the people would pray for guidance and protection for one another, almost by invoking creation's graces:

The goodness of sea be thine,
The goodness of earth be thine,
The goodness of heaven be thine.[1]

Not only was creation regarded as essentially good, despite its harshness and destructive potential, but there was also a sense of God's grace being released through love of the elements:

The grace of the love of the skies be thine,
The grace of the love of the stars be thine,
The grace of the love of the moon be thine,
The grace of the love of the sun be thine.[2]

The people believed that the grace of healing had been implanted within the goodness of creation, too. There is a story of a woman from the Island of Harris who suffered from a type of skin disease and was exiled from the community to live alone on the seashore. There she collected plants and shellfish and, having boiled them for eating, washed her sores with the remaining liquid. In time she was cured. She saw the grace of healing as having come to her through creation and so she prayed:

There is no plant in the ground
But is full of His virtue,
There is no form in the strand
But is full of His blessing.

Jesu! Jesu! Jesu!
Jesu who ought to be praised.

There is no life in the sea,
There is no creature in the river,
There is naught in the firmament,
But proclaims His goodness.
Jesu! Jesu! Jesu!
Jesu who ought to be praised.

There is no bird on the wing,
There is no star in the sky,
There is nothing beneath the sun,
But proclaims His goodness.
Jesu! Jesu! Jesu!
Jesu who ought to be praised.[3]

The life of God was viewed as being deep within creation as well as being distinct from it. A prayer of God's enfolding, clearly modelled on the ancient 'Breastplate' hymn of St Patrick which celebrates Christ in all things, put it this way:

The Three who are over me,
The Three who are below me,
The Three who are above me here,
The Three who are above me yonder;
The Three who are in earth,
The Three who are in air,
The Three who are in heaven,
The Three who are in the great pouring sea.[4]

These prayers celebrate the presence of God in the elements, but do not confuse God with creation and are therefore not pantheistic, although superficial or unsympathetic observers sometimes reached this conclusion. The prayers distinguish creation from the

Creator, between the Source of life and living things, and
express the desire to be true to God:

> Grant Thou to me, Father beloved,
> From whom each thing that is freely flows,
> That no tie over-strict, no tie over-dear,
> May be between myself and this world below.[5]

This spirituality was able to unite a distinction between
God and creation with a great reverence for creation's
elements. The reverencing of creation without deifying
it was particularly notable in the people's relationship
to the sun and moon. In the Hebrides, until well into
the last century it was the custom for men to take off
their cap to the sun in the morning and for women to
bend the knee to the moon at night. An old woman of
Barra explained the practice to Carmichael in the following terms: 'I think myself that it is a matter for
thankfulness, the golden-bright sun of virtues giving us
warmth and light by day, and the white moon of the
seasons giving us guidance and leading by night.'[6]

In the islands, where the need for sunshine for the
crops was recognized and the moon and stars were
viewed as guiding the fishermen at night, a sharp
awareness of the gift of physical light is understandable,
but some of the ritual attached to it moves beyond a
simple thanksgiving towards the type of nature mysticism the old Celtic Church had accepted into its
spirituality. The practice of dancing in the moonlight
out in the hills and singing prayers to the moon worried
those who did not also recognize in it a form of Christ
mysticism. Members of the wider Church felt that it
was superstitious to make acts of reverence to the new
moon and address it directly while simultaneously
making the sign of the cross over the heart. This was

not the sort of behaviour associated with John Knox in Edinburgh, for instance, or Thomas Cranmer in Canterbury, but occasionally such practices did find their way even into England; similar rituals can of course be found in the Celtic fringes of Cornwall, Wales and Ireland. There is a delightful story of a girl from the west coast of Scotland who, on moving to England, continued her habit of bowing to the moon as a sign of respect for the light of God within it. Her father, however, who was an Episcopalian priest, is said to have paid her to discontinue the practice lest the bishop came to hear about it.

A wonderful aspect of this reverence for the sun and moon was the way in which the attention of the person praying would move back and forth, almost like the shuttle of a loom, between the physical and the spiritual. Worshippers gave thanks for the material gift of light while at the same time being aware of the spiritual light of God within creation. Many of the 'sun' prayers, for instance (including the following example) demonstrate this:

The eye of the great God,
The eye of the God of glory,
The eye of the King of hosts,
The eye of the King of the living,
Pouring upon us
At each time and season,
Pouring upon us
Gently and generously.
Glory to thee,
Thou glorious sun.
Glory to thee, thou sun,
Face of the God of life.[7]

Such prayers convey a sense of the spiritual coming to us in and through the physical. An old man from Arasaig used to bow and say a prayer to the setting sun and then continue:

> I am in hope that the great and gracious God
> Will not put out for me the light of grace
> Even as thou dost leave me this night.[8]

This tradition also includes the practice, typical of many of the Psalms in the Scriptures, of seeing our voices as joining the voice of the whole universe in giving praise to God. Ours is but a strain, and in terms of the evolution of the earth a very late strain indeed, in the great song of creation, a song that was sung for millions of years before the advent of humanity. It is a song that continues to be sung by the waves of the sea and the breath of the wind, even while we sleep at night or are distracted from our awareness of God. A common practice in the Western Isles, especially among the old, was to intone their prayers while listening to the sea along the shore, so that their voices might join 'the voicing of the waves' and their praises 'the praises of the ceaseless sea'.[9] As one old woman told Carmichael, she had been instructed since her youth to pray constantly and to see her prayer as joining creation's unending song:

> My mother would be asking us to sing our morn-ing song to God down in the back-house, as Mary's lark was singing it up in the clouds, and as Christ's mavis [song-thrush] was singing it yonder in the tree, giving glory to the God of the creatures for the repose of the night, for the light of the day, and for the joy of life. She would tell us that every

creature on the earth here below and in the ocean beneath and in the air above was giving glory to the great God of the creatures and the worlds, of the virtues and the blessings, and would *we* be dumb! My dear mother. . . . My heart loves the earth in which my beloved mother rests.[10]

Alongside this emphasis on the goodness of creation, the prayers convey a tremendous earthiness. In a blessing for the house, for instance, there is an unabashed asking for 'plenty of food, plenty of drink, plenty of beds, and plenty of ale'.[11] Life was seen as having been created good, very good, and the people had no hesitation in looking to God at times of festivity and fun. Many of the night benedictions, for instance, ask for a blessing on 'the bed-companion of my love',[12] and others for Christ's blessing on their 'virile sons and conceptive daughters'.[13] One of the most lovely, in its uninhibited inclusion of sexual attraction into prayer, is that by Isobel, the fifteenth-century Duchess of Argyll, who prayed:

There is a youth comes wooing me,
O King of kings, may he succeed!
Would he were stretched upon my breast,
With his body against my skin.[14]

Hardly the sort of prayer that we could imagine John Calvin saying, let alone Mrs Calvin.

The emphasis in these prayers on the goodness of earth and the belief that God's dwelling-place is deep within creation is a further reflection and development of the interweaving of the spiritual and the material exemplified by the art of the old Celtic Church, where the patterns of heaven and earth intertwine and overlap.

So to look to God is not to look away from life but to look more deeply into it. Together with this emphasis on the presence of God at the heart of creation, of God being the heartbeat of life, there is also a sense of the closeness, the personal immediacy of God to us, a closeness not only of God but of the whole host of heaven, enfolding the earth and its people with love. Celtic belief does not thereby become a sentimental piety; rather, there exists in it and in its prayers a readiness to give and receive warm affection in relation to Christ and his saints and angels. As well as being referred to as 'King of the Elements', Christ is named as 'King of Tenderness'. God is seen as encompassing us with a gentleness of strength and care:

> God to enfold me,
> God to surround me,
> God in my speaking,
> God in my thinking.
>
> God in my sleeping,
> God in my waking,
> God in my watching,
> God in my hoping.
>
> God in my life,
> God in my lips,
> God in my soul,
> God in my heart.
>
> God in my sufficing,
> God in my slumber,
> God in mine ever-living soul,
> God in mine eternity.[15]

The saints and angels were viewed as immediately present, at both the critical moments of life and death and in the most ordinary times of daily work and routine. They are fondly addressed and regarded as messengers of God's everlasting love for us. Approaching death, one old woman, for instance, prayed, 'O Mary of grace, mayest thou give me thy two arms around mine everlasting soul when going over the black river of death'.[16] Often 'the sainted women of heaven', as they were called, would be portrayed almost as midwives of the life that is to come, stretching out their arms to receive us and to welcome us at the end, and guiding us in our lives:

> The love and affection of the angels be to you,
> The love and affection of the saints be to you,
> The love and affection of heaven be to you,
> To guard you and to cherish you.[17]

The saints were always present to guide and to guard, though sometimes with an intimacy that seems almost too close for comfort. Not only are Matthew, Mark, Luke and John viewed in some of the prayers as being at the four corners of our bed, but Columba is on our pillow and Brigid under the covers!

The mark of Celtic spirituality that had appeared first, and been stressed by Pelagius, was that of the image of God at the heart of the human. There was the conviction, and it features again in these prayers, that to look into the face of a newborn child is to see the image of God. 'The lovely likeness of the Lord is in thy pure face,' is a phrase in one of the invocations of blessing on a child. It was believed that by looking deeply enough into any human face, not just that of a child, we may glimpse the image of God, although often, maybe even usually, it is covered over by marks of sin and confusion.

In the Western Isles there developed a practice of

prayer and blessing at the birth of a child by the mid-wives, or 'womb-women', as they were called. These prayers clearly reflect the conviction that the life at the heart of each person is begotten of God. As one mid-wife put it, the newborn child comes 'from the bosom of the everlasting Father'[18], and so the child was seen as bearing the freshness of God's image. The midwife also used to put water on the baby's forehead as part of the blessing. This was called 'the birth baptism', as opposed to the 'priestly' baptism, the sacrament that would be celebrated later (and sometimes it was much later, because of the large number of islands that a parish priest or minister had to cover). One midwife told Carmichael that when 'the image of the God of life is born into the world' she would put three drops of water on the child's forehead and say:

The little drop of the Father
On thy little forehead, beloved one.

The little drop of the Son
On thy little forehead, beloved one.

The little drop of the Spirit
On thy little forehead, beloved one. . . .

To keep thee for the Three,
To shield thee, to surround thee;

To save thee for the Three,
To fill thee with the graces;

The little drop of the Three
To lave thee with the graces.[19]

In these prayers, as in the early stream of Celtic spiri-tuality, God's gift of grace is regarded not as planting something totally new in essentially bad soil, but as bringing out or releasing the goodness which is present in the soil of human life but obstructed by evil. Grace is seen as enabling our nature to flourish, as co-operating with the light that is within every person. Thus many of the prayers for grace ask for the development of aspects of our essential, God-given nature. For example, they request 'the grace of health', 'the grace of love' and the grace of wisdom, beauty, voice, music or dancing. One prayer of blessing includes these lines:

A voice soft and musical I pray for thee,
And a tongue loving and mild:
Two things good for daughter and for son,
For husband and for wife.
The joy of God be in thy face,
Joy to all who see thee.[20]

This emphasis on essential goodness did not obscure a sharp awareness of evil or the need constantly to guard against it. Many of the prayers are in fact pleas for protection:

I am placing my soul and my body
Under thy guarding this night, O Brigid,
O calm Fostermother of the Christ without sin,
O calm Fostermother of the Christ of wounds.

I am placing my soul and my body
Under thy guarding this night, O Mary,
O tender Mother of the Christ of the poor,
O tender Mother of the Christ of tears.

I am placing my soul and my body
Under thy guarding this night, O Christ,
O Thou Son of the tears, of the wounds, of the
    piercings,
May Thy cross this night be shielding me.

51

I am placing my soul and my body
Under Thy guarding this night, O God,
O Thou Father of help to the poor feeble pilgrims,
Protector of earth and of heaven,
Protector of earth and of heaven.[21]

What is it that happened to this beautiful tradition of
prayer, this flowering of Celtic spirituality that bloomed
long after the branch of the Celtic Church had been
severed? It seems that formal opposition to these
prayers began in the sixteenth century. The Scottish
Reformation, with its emphatically Augustinian–
Calvinistic theology, had little sympathy with the Celtic
spirituality of the Western Isles. It was generally felt
that the people of the islands were 'little better than
pagan until the Reformation'.[22] The neo-Calvinism
of the seventeenth century – particularly that associated
with the Westminster Confession (approved by Parlia-
ment in 1648 as the authorized 'Confession of Faith
for the three Kingdoms') which accentuated Calvin's
theory of total human depravity – only increased the
antipathy of the wider Church towards a spirituality
that celebrated the goodness of creation and God's
image in the human. The ancient stories and legends of
the islands concerning Brigid and other Celtic saints
were now called 'lies' by the established Church.

The evangelical revival of the eighteenth and nineteenth centuries continued the emphasis on original sin
and further widened the perceived division between
spirit and matter, between the sacred and the secular.
Its Sabbatarianism and its doctrine of election drove a
wedge between the so-called holy place of the Church
and the holy day of the Sabbath and the rest of life, and
similarly between the holy people, the saved ones, and

the rest of humankind, the damned ones. It was a
repressive religiosity. In the islands, young men and
women were being kept apart at weddings; the old songs
and stories, music and dances had been banned, and the
musicians' pipes and fiddles were being collected and
burned, often by the Church's ministers. Roosters were
even being locked away on the Sabbath, for fear that *ha!*
they might do something natural with the hens.

The repression was of Celtic spirituality in its broad-
est sense, for it touched the culture and language of the
people as much as their religious life: schoolteachers
beat children for speaking Gaelic and the ministers
inhibited people from openly reciting the old prayers.
As one young woman recounted for Carmichael, she
and some other girls had begun to sing a Gaelic song
as they walked home after school one day. 'The schoolmaster heard us,' she said, 'and called us back. He
punished us till the blood trickled from our fingers,
although we were big girls, with the dawn of woman-
hood upon us.'23 Carmichael tells many stories about
how hesitant the people often were to divulge the old
prayers to him, lest they be overheard or found out by
the schoolmaster or parish minister. Sometimes people
would wait until he left their village and follow him,
perhaps under the cover of night, to the next village, in
order to tell him the old stories and prayers in safety.
Even then they were cautious; Carmichael describes
how some would flee his room if there was a knock at
the door, leaving hats and coats behind in their hurry
to escape.

What was it the establishment feared in this stream
of spirituality that ran so deep within the people of
the Celtic world? Was it in part that people of such a
spirituality could not be neatly controlled or confined

within the narrow bounds of religion and order as defined by the established Church and society of the day? Are people who believe that the life of God is deep within them easily cowed or brought into line? It is difficult to know exactly what, over the centuries, sparked off the fear of Pelagius and Eriugena, for instance, rousing the might of Church and State to act against them and against those who followed them. However, in the case of the people of the Western Isles, although the religious establishment tried to suppress the old prayers, the most decisive blow against their continued use was probably struck by the Highland Clearances of the first half of the nineteenth century. The clearances were not of course a Church policy, but when tens of thousands of people were torn from their lands and islands and separated from clan and family, there was virtually no official Church resistance. In fact, in many cases, the opposite was true. The parish minister was often the voice and pawn of the powerful.

1792 was known as 'The Year of the Sheep', in which many of the great landowners of Scotland began to introduce sheep by the thousands, expelling crofters in almost equal numbers, to free the land for grazing. The sale of wool was more profitable than leasing the land to the people for the traditional small-scale family farming that had characterized the Highlands and Islands for centuries. In the centres of power, like London and Edinburgh, the clearances were euphemistically called 'Land Improvements'. For the people affected it meant the destruction of their culture, their way of life and the context of their spirituality. Many of the old simply became homeless and many of the young died of disease in the move to the cities and abroad. One old woman described to Carmichael some of the terrible things she had witnessed:

> Many a thing I have seen in my own day and generation. Many a thing, O Mary Mother of the black sorrow! I have seen the townships swept, and the big holdings being made of them, the people being driven out of the countryside to the streets of Glasgow and to the wilds of Canada, such of them as did not die of hunger and plague and smallpox while going across the ocean. I have seen the women putting the children in the carts which were being sent from Benbecula ... while their husbands lay bound in the pen and were weeping beside them, without power to give them a helping hand, though the women themselves were crying aloud and their little children wailing like to break their hearts. I have seen the big strong men, the champions of the countryside, the stalwarts of the world, being bound on Loch Boisdale quay and cast into the ship as would be done to a batch of horses or cattle in the boat, the bailiffs and the ground-officers and the constables and the policemen gathered behind them in pursuit of them. The God of life and He only knows all the loathsome work of men on that day.[24]

With the scattering of family and the loss of land, livelihood and a distinct way of life (including, for instance, the gatherings or 'ceilidhs' in which the old stories and songs had been recited and passed down), there came an inevitable loss of memory. Nearly all of the prayers in this stream of spirituality had been orally communicated from generation to generation; now many of them began to be forgotten. Carmichael was aware that he was collecting the prayers at the verge of their disappearance from living history. Something other than a loss of collective memory had occurred for many of those who remained, however. It was as if something of their spirituality had been broken in the collapse of the simplicity and wholeness of their lives. One old man recounted to Carmichael what life had been like before the clearances, when four generations of a family could sometimes be found dancing together on the hillside:

> But the clearances came upon us, destroying all, turning our small crofts into big farms for the stranger, and turning our joy into misery, our gladness into bitterness, our blessing into blasphemy, and our Christianity into mockery. . . . The tears come on my eyes when I think of all we suffered and of the sorrows.[25]

One can wonder about the wrong done to these people and why it happened. One must wonder also why there was so little effective resistance from them to the clearances. And why was it that their spirituality was so shaken? Was it in part because it was a spirituality without a church, so that when family and culture were decimated there was no structure or context left in which the treasuries of their spirituality could be protected and passed on? This is not to say that nothing of this stream of spirituality survived, for, as we shall see, it was to find new courses, but by the time Carmichael made his collection the ancient prayers were being used by a decreasing number of men and women, a dwindling remnant of a strong and deep spiritual tradition. If Carmichael had not transcribed

them, most of the prayers would have been erased from
memory within another generation and a rich mine of
spirituality for us and for the whole Church today
would have been lost.

One of the most beautiful aspects of the prayers of
the Western Isles is the perspective that death is a river
that is hard to see or a place of black sorrow that is
difficult to cross and that the angels of God are guiding
us over to a goodness of unimaginable glory. This glory
is not, however, unrelated to the goodness we have
known in creation and in the earth's cycles of seasons.
Rather, it is a return to the very home of the seasons,
to the Source of creation, a returning to the One who
is the heart of all life. A prayer that was said at the
deathbed of a loved one speaks of the depth of hope
found in this tradition, not only for an individual in the
face of death, but for a whole people, and even for the
whole of creation:

Thou goest home this night to thy home of winter,
To thy home of autumn, of spring, and of summer;
Thou goest home this night to thy perpetual home,
To thine eternal bed, to thine eternal slumber. . . .

Sleep this night in the breast of thy Mother,
Sleep, thou beloved, while she herself soothes thee;
Sleep thou this night on the Virgin's arm,
Sleep, thou beloved, while she herself kisses thee.

The great sleep of Jesus, the surpassing sleep of
    Jesus,
The sleep of Jesus' wound, the sleep of Jesus' grief,
The young sleep of Jesus, the restoring sleep of
    Jesus,
The sleep of the kiss of Jesus of peace and of
    glory. . . .

The shade of death lies upon thy face, beloved,
But the Jesus of grace has His hand round about
    thee;
In nearness to the Trinity farewell to thy pains,
Christ stands before thee and peace is in His mind.

Sleep, O sleep in the calm of all calm,
Sleep, O sleep in the guidance of guidance,
Sleep, O sleep in the love of all loves;
Sleep, O beloved, in the Lord of life,
Sleep, O beloved, in the God of life![26]

4 ❖ Listening with the Imagination:
George MacDonald

The Celtic culture and spirituality of the people of the Western Isles had been torn and displaced by a combination of adverse factors. Speaking and singing in the Gaelic had been forcibly discouraged and the Church had actively suppressed the old prayers and music and customs, fearing that they sprang from pre-Christian and pantheistic ways. The Clearances, as we have seen, caused further fragmentation. At the same time, the theology of the established religion was expressing an extreme form of Calvinism, with its conviction that the image of God in the human had been totally erased by Adam's fall. 'Mankind,' declared the Church of Scotland's Confession of Faith, 'is wholly defiled in all parts and faculties of soul and body . . . utterly indisposed, disabled, and made opposite to all good, and wholly inclined to all evil.'[1]

It is difficult to imagine a spirituality more starkly opposed to Celtic spirituality's emphasis on our essential goodness. It is even harder to imagine what was happening in the mind and soul of a mother looking into the face of her newborn child and being told he or she was 'wholly defiled'. Similarly, men of the Church were being encouraged to believe that their unbaptized neighbours and people of other faiths were at heart entirely opposed to goodness. So closed was this form of extreme Calvinism, combined as it was with a rigid belief in predestination, that even well into the nineteenth century there was considerable opposition within Scotland to foreign mission; it was considered futile to preach the gospel to people predestined to be damned for their essential sinfulness. This may be difficult for most of us to comprehend today, but within the major traditions of Western Christianity we have been influenced by aspects of this Calvinist and Augustinian stream of spirituality that denies an essential goodness at the heart of every person. There is much in the Western tradition that has discouraged us from believing and hoping that, even in the midst of terrible wrong and evil, deeper still, buried maybe, at the core of every human being is the image of God.

Despite the excessive and militant Calvinism of early nineteenth-century Scotland, the spring of Celtic spirituality continued to well up and find new forms of expression. Around the same time as Carmichael was collecting the prayers of an increasingly dispersed tradition in the Western Isles, another Scot, George MacDonald (1824–1905), was finding a new channel of expression for this ancient stream of spirituality and communicating it in the form of short stories and novels. Although MacDonald was born in Aberdeenshire, his family was part of the Western Isles clan and claimed relationship with the great Flora MacDonald who aided Bonny Prince Charlie to escape through the Hebrides after the defeat of the Highlanders in

1745. MacDonald was reared on the old Celtic stories and legends of the West and in time allowed these to shape the spirituality that he was to express through his fictional works. Many of his stories have been read particularly by the young, but he claimed to write for the 'childlike', both young and old, that is, for those who see with the eyes of a child. His works of the imagination strove to recover the inner faculty of sight whereby God may be seen within us, among us and in all the things of creation.

One of MacDonald's best-known novels, *The Princess and the Goblin* (1872), a work that was later profoundly to affect the spirituality of men like G. K. Chesterton and C. S. Lewis, reflects the continuing themes of Celtic spirituality. It tells the story of a young princess living in a great country house. She discovers that in the house, in one of its remote attic rooms, is a beautiful woman, in whom the freshness of youth is combined with the wisdom of the ages. Although she has been present always, like a grandmother watching over the princess and her family, and has been known to the king and others before, the princess meets her for the first time early in the story. She sits spinning a thread of light that is woven through all things, and which she instructs the young princess to hold wherever she is in order to feel her presence and be led to her. Others in the house see neither the beautiful woman nor her thread of light, and her room, which is to the young princess the most wonderful of places, filled with the scent of wild roses and the sound of the world's flowing waters, is to others merely an empty attic, dusty and forsaken.

The eternal mother is present to nurture and to guide, but present too are terrible forces of darkness plotting destruction. Within the mountain on which the house is built, living in subterranean caves, are goblins that tunnel their way into the foundations of the house, threaten its safety and intend to take the princess captive. The goblins are neither human nor animal, but a distorted and evil combination of the two. In the end their evil is self-destructive. The flood they had planned for the destruction of the house is turned on them and on their caves. The princess, having followed the beautiful woman's thread, escapes safely and, although the foundations of her house have been shaken by evil, they are not destroyed.

MacDonald owed much of his spirituality of the imagination to a so-called 'heretic' of the nineteenth century, a man named Alexander John Scott (1805–66).[2] Scott in turn was indebted to the ninth-century John Scotus Eriugena, the great Celtic philosopher who had taught that the light at the heart of all life is God (see Chapter 2). Scott's belief that God's love is in and for all people was in sharp contrast to the prevailing Calvinist doctrine which saw God not as within creation but as infinitely separated from it. God's redemptive love was seen as being granted exclusively to the elect to implant within them a grace of light entirely opposed to their natural state at birth. Scott and MacDonald, on the other hand, saw God as immediately present in the whole of life. Everywhere, Scott maintained, can be found the ladder that connects heaven and earth, God and humanity, with angels of the eternal light ascending and descending upon it. As MacDonald put it, the grandmother figure, who represents the presence of God, is within our house, always near, whether we are aware of her or not, whether we know her or not. The image of a staircase or ladder leading unexpectedly from the most ordinary of contexts into an opening into the eternal, was a favourite of MacDonald's, similar to C. S. Lewis's Narnian wardrobe.

Scott had grown up in the west of Scotland, among people who had looked for God in the whole of life. He described them as listening for God in all things, 'in the growth of the tree, in the rising of the morning sun, in the stars at night, and in the moon'.[3] In their 'inmost being', he said, they knew a type of communion with the uncreated at the heart of creation. It was of supreme importance to perceive the interweaving of the spiritual and the material, of heaven and earth, time and eternity 'from year to year, from month to month, from hour to hour'. What he was describing, of course, is the sort of spirituality that we have seen reflected in Carmichael's *Carmina Gadelica*, the tradition of prayer among the people of the Western Isles that expressed itself in the most ordinary contexts of day-to-day life. Always, said Scott, 'there is the greatness that lies within and beneath the common'.[4] Everywhere, therefore, we can glimpse signs of the presence of God's life in and among us, for God, he believed, is 'the Being on which all being rests'.[5]

In 1831, when he was a young man, Scott had been unanimously deposed by the General Assembly of the Church of Scotland on a charge of heresy. At one level the debate focused on what he had called 'the negation of the gospel', that is, the Church's attempt to limit the love of God to the Church and, specifically, to the elect. At a deeper level the debate was about the attempt to limit the life of God, to keep the essence of God's life entirely separate from the world and from creation. According to the established Church, when God's grace was given, from afar, as it were, it was not to allow the image and likeness of God to well up from our inner depths. It was, rather, to form an entirely separate body comprising the elect of God (the Church), which was essentially unrelated to creation and the world, matter and humanity being regarded as 'fallen'.

Scott had been critical too of the Church's doctrine of ordination, for the similar reason that it gave the impression that ordained ministers had a greater presence of God's Spirit within them than the rest of humanity. In contrast, Scott emphasized that the realm of Christ encompasses not simply those who are ordained, christened or otherwise claimed by the Church but all life, for Christ is the Life of the world. The Spirit of God, he said, is 'impregnated' throughout the whole of creation.[6] Where there is life and goodness, there is God. God exists wherever there is love and creativity. Similarly, Scott was critical of the Church's Sabbatarianism, because it taught that only one day of the week is holy, instead of seeing that the whole of life is sacred, every day, every hour, every moment.

One of the primary marks of Celtic spirituality, its belief in the essential goodness of creation, is prominent in the works of Scott and MacDonald. They believed that the natural world is infinitely deep. Everything in creation has issued forth from the invisible and contains something of the unseen life of God. Otherwise it would cease to exist. Because God's life is like the heartbeat at the centre of life, pulsating within, sustaining all that is, MacDonald's princess is aware of and alert to the Soul of creation. She has a sense of relationship with it, for all created things are an expression of God for our souls to see and feel. God is forever communicating his life and love in and through the outward forms of creation. The young princess is portrayed as greeting the flowering fields in the morning and seeing the connection between the light and mystery of the night skies and the beauty and love of the grandmother. The one is an expression of the other.

Just as an infant comes to know his mother through form and colour, scent and sound, so we come to a knowledge of God through the universe. 'Those who have a child's heart,' said Scott, 'will own and welcome this.'[7] Again, the emphasis is on becoming like a child, recovering the inner faculties we were born with and using them to glimpse the presence of spirit in created matter. Scott underlined the need to regain our innate childlike way of seeing that becomes increasingly obscured by neglect throughout our lives. The gift of the imagination, which in a child is still uninhibited, allows creation to be a lens through which we may fleetingly bring into focus aspects of the eternal. The young princess in MacDonald's story is surrounded by people whose inner senses and imagination have become so dulled by lack of use that they believe there is nothing to see in the matter of creation. Their blindness is an omen of the materialism that was increasingly to grip the Western world as the nineteenth century progressed.

MacDonald and Scott were witnessing the industrialization of a country and with it a growing spiritual insensitivity whereby life came to be viewed in more and more limited material terms. Accelerating throughout Western culture were the early stages of the extreme materialism characteristic of the twentieth century, when value and meaning are attached largely to the external.

In the midst of the nineteenth century's growing materialism, Scott and MacDonald were communicating a vision of <u>the uncreated being present within creation</u>. The constituents of the created universe Scott viewed as being like the strings of a Scottish harp, the hand moving across them being that of God. Thus creation is the communication between ourselves and God. Our prayers and worship form part of the great ongoing hymn of the universe, the song the elements have been singing continuously, since long before our human voice found expression. Just as we join creation's voice when we give praise to God, so the movement and colour and sound of creation's elements can be the voice to which we listen in prayer. In the wind roaring through a great forest or in the colours of the sky at sunset we can perceive the sound and light of creation and find in them God's graces of healing and creativity. Echoing an image that had recurred in Celtic spirituality from as early as Pelagius' time, Scott described creation as 'a transparency through which the light of God can be seen'.[8]

Scott and MacDonald did not pretend that terrible and destructive forces are not to be found in creation, but they maintained that creation is essentially good and that deeper than any destructive capacity in it is the life-giving presence of God. As Eriugena had said centuries earlier, creation is essentially a theophany, a showing or revealing of God's Soul to our souls. This does not mean that everything we see in creation is good or of God. We still need to discern with inner sight what is the essence of God in creation, and therefore what is truest and most unshakeable in life. Like Eriugena, Scott and MacDonald were saying that we should look not only to the Scriptures and the Church to know God, but to creation as well as our religious inheritance. Scott urged us to hold a Bible in one hand but also to study God 'in that other volume', namely, the great and holy book of creation.[9] Just as when we listen to the Scriptures we hope to hear God's living and immediate Word to us, yet will also hear words of human failure and violence, so when we explore creation we will perceive suffering and cruelty at one level and, deeper still, the grace and boundless creativity of God.

Celtic spirituality, with its emphasis on the goodness of creation, has lent itself to being hijacked and misinterpreted by those in search of a romantic perspective on creation, one that avoids the powers of evil at work in our world and in ourselves. The principalities of darkness are scattered throughout the goodness of creation, in our nations and communities, forever threatening the well-being of our relationships, our minds and our souls. Evil is like a snake coiled up in the grass of our lives; at times it suddenly springs up, catching us off our guard, to tempt us to violence of heart and action. As in Jesus' parable of the wheat and tares, seeds of evil have been planted in the essentially good field of life. Any profound spirituality must take account of the evil in and around us and provide ways of growing in spite of it; at the same time it should equip us to address and do battle with the darkness in ourselves and in the world.

Scott and MacDonald, like those in the stream of Celtic spirituality before them, were prepared to name and confront the darkness while celebrating the light that is at the heart of life. In MacDonald's story, the goblins threaten the very foundations of the princess's house. This is not a superficial treatment of evil; it recognizes evil's potential for destruction, which sometimes emerges from the most hidden recesses of our lives. It can seem as though evil's reserves are limitless, like the bottomless abyss from which the dragon and legions of darkness arise in the Book of Revelation. Is this not sometimes our impression when we consider places in our world where almost unimaginable wrongs are committed, or when we go through times of deep confusion and despair?

As pervasive and fundamental as evil appears to be, the recurrent hope in Celtic spirituality is that the darkness cannot overcome God's essential light. It was this that led MacDonald to believe, for example, that in the end even Satan would repent and be restored to his original role of angel of light.

Scott and MacDonald, then, were aware of the shadows in us all and in the whole of creation and of the goblins that threaten our spiritual foundations. Their spirituality inspired and enabled them to become involved in some of the most imaginative attempts in nineteenth-century Britain to address the evils of injustice and inequality. In 1848 Scott was one of the founders of Christian Socialism, which made daring efforts (considering the climate of the times) to unite the principles of socialism, hitherto associated with atheism, and Christianity. Christianizing socialism and socializing Christianity, they believed, was the key to social well-being and unity. They were thereby trying to deal with some of the deepest sources of inequity in society.

The Christian Socialist movement established, among other radical innovations, working men's colleges in London and Manchester. This was a way of teaching and furthering the principles of co-operation that its members believed to be part of the essential wholeness of life as created by God. MacDonald was involved with the social reformer John Ruskin in a project to transform city dwellings, particularly in the over-crowded and ugly slums, in a way that would reflect what they called 'the divine proportion'. This related the scale and design of human dwellings to natural growth patterns and proportions. It was an extraordinary and far-sighted attempt to learn from creation at a time when industrialization was establishing patterns of ignoring and squandering creation, long before the dawn of twentieth-century ecological awareness.

The belief in the goodness of creation, ever present in the stream of Celtic spirituality, went hand in hand with a conviction that humanity bears within itself the image of God, maybe deeply buried but not erased. In an age when Highlanders were being cleared from their ancestral lands like cattle and the poor in the cities, living in overcrowded, disease-ridden conditions, were being treated as little better than slave labour, the Church's doctrine, which either reflected these wrongs or was partly responsible for them, was that at birth we are fallen creatures without a trace of the image of God in us. It was in this context that MacDonald in his works of the imagination was repeatedly using images of us all being princes and princesses. Whether we know it or not, and usually we don't, we are all of the grandmother, as it were. We may have forgotten our inner royal lineage. We may have forgotten that we have come from God, just as we forget our time in our mother's womb, but at the very core of our life we are begotten by God, his sons and daughters. This led MacDonald to question the traditional doctrine of creation out of nothing. Our souls, he said, have not come from nothing. Rather, as Eriugena had asserted long before, our life comes from the very substance of God's life.

As early as the 1830s, Scott had contended that God is not merely present 'beside the human, but in the human'.[10] The Church in Scotland did not even accept that God loves all people, let alone that he is the Life within all human life. The Infinite, said Scott, is 'consubstantiated with the human', so that what is most truly human is what is most divine. 'There is no part of our nature,' he declared, 'as God made it and means it, that is not brought into the dearest nearness to Himself'.[11] In other words, every human faculty and sense in its truest form, every pure human affection and good desire for life is essentially an expression of God's life, God's voice, God's desire, and to enter deeply enough into these truly human characteristics is to approach the very 'mind and being of God'. Again, the emphasis that comes across in Celtic spirituality and in this particular expression of it is that spirituality is not about looking away from life but more deeply into it, not about denying the human but about releasing our truest selves, and that the life of our truest self partakes of the very substance of God's life, the One Self that is at the heart of all selves. In Christ, the perfect image of God, we see our truest self.

Part of this emphasis within the Celtic tradition of the image of God being at the heart of the human is the conviction that the divine image is more profound than any outward distinction and division between men and women. As St Paul had said, in Christ essentially there is neither male nor female. To be made in the image of God is to share fundamentally in the Unity that underlies life rather than being defined primarily in terms of the distinctions of race and colour and sex that are outward and varied manifestations of the One Life. In Celtic spirituality this led to the further freedom of being able to use either male or female images to describe God. Just as the Bible uses a wide range of imagery, both masculine and feminine, to refer to God, so in Celtic spirituality a mother's heart could be imagined at the heart of God, or God's love perceived as that of a father. MacDonald's story, clearly reflective of this tradition, used the grandmother as an image of feminine beauty and wisdom to represent the divine. Thus the feminine becomes a rich symbol of the One who gives birth to life, and who nurtures and watches over creation like a mother her child.

MacDonald came to understand that the attraction between the sexes, and the attraction between masculine and feminine, was so essential to life and to its continuity and fruitfulness, that it must also manifest something of the nature of God. The desire for union, for a coming together between masculine and feminine, and the yearning for creativity and giving birth, which are fundamental to the goodness of creation, are reflective of God at the very heart of life. This spirituality, by not limiting itself to masculine images of God, opened itself to the rich realm of feminine imagery and the even richer realm beyond, where these images intermingle, to communicate the creativity of the Unknowable. This made room for an awareness of the essential goodness of the sexual, and indeed of everything that is truest of our life and creativity. In our secular–materialist age with its obsessions with the outward and the physical, the problem, it seems, is not our interest in sexuality, which is essentially God-given and good, but rather a fascination with it in a way that distorts our sexual desires and prevents them from being a manifestation of God's passion for self-giving and commitment and creativity. The result is that we play with sexuality at the surface of life rather than seeing that our deepest desires, given by God, rise out of the profoundest depths of life. Our sexual energies reflect, in their goodness, God's yearnings for intimacy, creative expression and new life.

In the case of Scott and MacDonald, awareness that both the feminine and the masculine reflect the image of God, gave rise to practical as well as literary and theological expression. In 1848, for instance, Scott had become one of the founders and first professors of Bedford College in London, the first centre of higher education for women in Britain based on the principles of religious freedom. Graduates of Bedford College were to initiate some of the reforming movements for women's political equality in Britain. MacDonald, especially during his years in Manchester, also promoted further education for women. He and Scott, like Pelagius in the early days of Celtic spirituality, had no doubt that women had the same natural right to education as men. They saw the beauty of the image of God in both and regarded education as playing a significant part in liberating the goodness of that image in people's lives and relationships.

In Scott and MacDonald the Celtic stream of spirituality was taken into the realms of literature, education and political concern, but for the most part it was still a spirituality without a church, without a clearly defined religious home. Scott had been deposed from the Church of Scotland ministry as a young man. In his English exile he gathered around him inquiring and like-minded souls, but they prayed and worshipped on the fringes of the major religious traditions rather than within them. His relationship to the Church was largely that of a dissident. Similarly, MacDonald had been forced out of the Congregational ministry, criticized and misunderstood, and for the rest of his life remained on the edge of traditional religion, but by the time Scott died in 1866 there were signs of a coming change. Many of the young men who had studied under or consulted Scott, and had absorbed much of his vision and spirituality, later became leaders of the Church in Britain. John Tulloch and Norman MacLeod, for instance, had a great impact on the spirituality of the Scottish Church in years to come, freeing it from much of its enclosed Calvinism and opening it again to life and to the world, and English Nonconformism was influenced by the spirituality of men like David Simon, James Baldwin Brown and James Picton, all of whom as young men had been guided by Scott. J. Picton, in his controversial work *The Mystery of Matter* (1878), further developed Scott's emphasis on the sacredness of creation and was consequently accused, like so many before him in the Celtic tradition, of pantheism. However, it was MacDonald's novels that had the greatest impact in both England and Scotland. Within a very few years of being written they found acceptance among both the laity and the clergy in the major traditions and opened a side door for Celtic spirituality's re-entry into the Church.

5 ✤ Listening and Acting:
George MacLeod

One of the younger Scottish ministers who had been influenced by Alexander Scott, and who in time became a great promoter of George MacDonald's novels, was Norman MacLeod (1812–72). He exercised an enormous influence on the spirituality of the Scottish Church in the middle of the nineteenth century. In the 1843 Disruption, which split the Established Church of Scotland over the issue of patronage, he chose to remain within the National Church for the sake of unity. He brought to his Church leadership the characteristically Celtic trait of seeking God's presence in the whole of life instead of almost exclusively within the Church and its traditions.

Perhaps one of the greatest of MacLeod's contributions to Scottish spirituality was his work to liberate it from the legalistic Sabbatarianism which had insisted, for instance, that on Sundays, 'the Lord's Day', the Edinburgh Botanic Gardens should be closed and trains should not be allowed to run. MacLeod's intention was not just to criticize, like Alexander Scott earlier in the century, Scottish Sabbatarianism and its attempt to set apart one day as holy rather than seeing the whole of life as sacred. He also wanted to express the belief that the world was God's dwelling-place, to assert that the whole of creation bore within itself the renewing graces of God. These were not confined to the Church and its Scriptures and sacraments. Furthermore, to allow Sunday travel and leisure was a moral issue, for the vast majority of workers had only one day off a week, and that was Sunday. They were essentially being denied access to the country and, in the city, to one of Edinburgh's most beautiful places of nature. The successful campaign to open the Botanic Gardens on Sundays was a sign of a spirituality that went beyond the four walls of the Church. It reflected an aspect of the Celtic stream of spirituality's practice of listening for the heartbeat of God in the whole of life.

MacLeod became Moderator of the General Assembly of the Church of Scotland in 1869, only three years after Scott's death, but, more significantly, less than 40 years since Scott had been condemned for heresy. A tremendous shift in spirituality had occurred over a very brief span of time. This is not to say that everything suddenly changed, but rather that British Christianity was beginning to rediscover the ancient Celtic way of seeing that for centuries had been forced to the very edges of the Church.

Norman MacLeod played a significant part in the beginnings of that rediscovery, but the figure who most clearly embodied it and who reunited the two ways of seeing, torn apart for centuries, was Norman MacLeod's grandson, George Fielden MacLeod (1895–1991).[1] He taught that we should look for God not away from the material world in some spiritual realm but rather more deeply in the life of the world. The spiritual is not opposed to the physical, he believed, for God is to be found in the material realm of creation, not in an escape from it.[2] For that reason, as he liked to say, 'matter matters', whether that be the matter of our physical bodies, the matter of creation or the matter of bodies politic, because the spiritual is to be found at the heart of the material.

Similarly, in relation to the tendency to distance God's life from our life, MacLeod emphasized the fact that we are in touch with God every moment that we live, 'for the simple reason that God is life: not religious life, nor Church life, but the whole [of] life. . . . God is the Life of life.'[3] Spiritual awareness, then, was about being aware of God in the midst of the change and movement and flow of life, in the rising of the morning sun, in the work and relationships of daily life, in the great struggles of society and nation, in alertness to the interior life of the soul, in times of rest and sleep and even dreaming. God is at the heart of all life, in both the visible and invisible. We don't have to try to reach God through acts of devotion, for God is closer to us than our very breath. 'We have been given union with God whether we like it or not,' MacLeod said. 'Our flesh is his flesh, and we can't jump out of our skins.'[4] This was not pantheism. It was rather to believe, like Scott, Eriugena and other Celts before him, that God is the Being on which all being rests, the Light within all light, the Life at the heart of all that has life.

Who was this man who managed to hold together the mystical perspective of Celtic spirituality and his ministry in the established Church of Scotland? George MacLeod is known for many things and perhaps mainly for his peace activism, but his greatness lies in having brought Celtic spirituality's way of seeing back into the Church's formal life. Of course, this does not mean that suddenly there came a balance between the traditions that had clashed at Whitby, between the St John tradition, which listened for God in all things, and the St Peter tradition, which heard the Word of God primarily within the Church. The struggle, represented historically by the seventh-century conflict between the Celtic mission and the Roman mission, did not come to an abrupt end. However, a leader within British Christianity was now living in a creative tension between these two ways of seeing.

MacLeod was both a Celtic mystic and a Presbyterian minister, and proud of it. He liked to ask people, for instance, what the anagram of Presbyterian is. 'The anagram of Presbyterian,' he would tell them, 'is "best in prayer".' He would go on to ask what the anagram of Episcopal is, and say, 'The anagram of Episcopal is "Pepsi Cola".' It was with this delicacy of touch that MacLeod handled ecumenical relations. Not that he spared Presbyterians, either. As nearly everyone who met him in Scotland will remember, one of the first questions he would ask was, 'Are you a Presbyterian or a Christian?' Or he would say, 'Why do Presbyterian ministers speak longer than other men?' and then give the answer: 'They don't; it just seems longer.' This was his humorous way of encouraging people not to take too seriously the religious boundaries by which we so often define ourselves. MacLeod constantly used laughter to show others a new way of seeing, particularly the perception that God is the Life of the world and not merely some religious aspect of it.

George MacLeod was born in 1895 into a family that was probably the greatest ecclesiastical dynasty in Scotland. The MacLeods of Morvern on the west coast had given more than 550 years of ordained service to the established Church. MacLeod's was a privileged as well as an ecclesiastical family. He had childhood memories, for instance, of a written menu for the evening meal and being waited on by maids. His background was broadened by periods of study in England, at Winchester and Oxford. When the First World War came he served as an officer with the Argyll and Sutherland Highlanders, seeing heavy fighting on the Western Front, and his bravery won him the Military Cross and the *Croix de Guerre*.

The war profoundly affected MacLeod. He witnessed, as did so many, the slaughter of friends and companions. So shaken was he by what he saw that he later described himself as falling apart at this point. Going through half a bottle of whisky and 50 cigarettes a day, 'I was going to hell in a hurry,' he said. But as he travelled back to the front after a leave of absence, MacLeod reached a critical turning-point in his life. Not even waiting until the train reached its destination, he knelt down in the railway compartment and gave himself to Christ. It was typical of the man to act as soon as he had heard within himself the compelling truth that he needed to change.

It was of course years before he understood many of the implications of his sudden conversion experience in the railway carriage, but after the war MacLeod trained for the Church of Scotland ministry. His father was a Presbyterian, his mother a Quaker, and during his years at Winchester he had been confirmed as an Anglican, so he now described himself as 'a walking ecumenical disaster'. After training for the ministry he became Assistant Minister at St Giles' in Edinburgh, Scotland's principal Cathedral, and then Collegiate Minister at the prestigious Church of St Cuthbert's where he was a very popular preacher. But increasingly he became aware of what he called 'the two nations' of his country, the rich and the poor. So disturbed was he by this division that in 1930 he accepted, to the surprise of the establishment, a call to the Parish of Govan, the shipbuilding area in Glasgow marked in the hungry thirties by severe unemployment and widespread poverty.

It was during this period that MacLeod moved from a fairly straightforward form of High Presbyterianism towards a more mystical as well as a more political spirituality. This combination of the mystical and the political is what is so remarkable about MacLeod. The true mark of Christian spirituality, he now declared, 'is to get one's teeth into things. . . . Painstaking service to humankind's most material needs is the essence of Christian spirituality.'[5] In other words, to move more deeply into life, and especially into its places of struggle and suffering, like those he was seeing in Glasgow, is to move closer to the life of Christ, the light that is within even the darkest of situations. The word 'spiritual', he believed, was often dangerously misunderstood. People generally imagine that 'to go mystical', as he put it, is to turn away from the affairs of the world. It is rather to go more deeply into life, to find God at the heart of life, deeper than any wrong, and to liberate God's goodness within us and in our relationships, both individually and collectively.

MacLeod tended to see books on spirituality, prayer life, spiritual exercises, etc. as forming what he called 'the bankrupt corner' of his library. The truth is that MacLeod probably regarded most of his library as bankrupt. He was not a scholar and often skipped pretty lightly over historical detail. This does not mean that he was unaware of some of the main literary sources of Celtic spirituality, such as the *Carmina Gadelica* and the works of George MacDonald, but he was clearly not tempted away from action by study. Instead, he was always drawn to be part of the immediate flow of life, and intuitively to grasp in his normal daily routine the Life that is within all life and at the heart of every moment. He wrote:

> It is the primacy of God as Now that we must recover in Christian mysticism. . . . When in the morning we get to our desk, that list of meetings, the whole design of the day's life as it builds up from this or that telephone call, the person we like whom we are to meet at four, the person more difficult to like who will come at five. . . . Get through the day we are apt to say, and then perhaps at nine o'clock tonight, or nearer perhaps to eleven, we can have our time with God.

MacLeod, quoting George MacDonald, affirmed, '*Whatever* wakes my heart and mind, thy presence is, my Lord.' Our innumerable 'nows' are our points of contact with God.[6]

One of MacLeod's most moving accounts about the importance of being aware and alert to the present concerns his daughter's first day at school. It speaks of the experience we have all had, at different points in life, of missing the moment:

> I was busy. I was writing letters. I was self-important. My little daughter was going to school that morning for the first time. She came into my room, in her first school uniform. I said, 'Your tie is not quite straight.' Then I looked at her eyes. She wasn't crying. She was unutterably disappointed. She hadn't come for tie inspection. She had come

to show she was going to school for the first time.
A terrific day, and I had let her down. What is that
bit in the Gospel? Whosoever shall offend against
one of these little ones . . . better for a millstone
to be tied around his neck and that he be cast into
the sea. I ran downstairs. I said all the right things.
I crossed the road with her. I went to school with
her. I had missed the moment, missed the point. I
will always see these eyes. Sometimes when I am
very busy. Sometimes when I am writing letters. I
am forgiven, but I won't forget.[7]

Although MacLeod emphasized a spirituality of awareness, a looking and listening in the midst of every
moment of life, this is not to say that he did not believe
in setting aside time for formal private and communal
prayer. He believed in this strongly and was committed
to it with an almost puritanical zeal. He also taught
others strictly to practise the habit of prayer in their
daily life. However, what most debilitates our prayer
life, he asserted, is not bad prayer technique. It is 'our
presupposition that the pressures of life are on one side
while God is on some other side'.[8] For MacLeod, it
was precisely at the pressure points of life that God is
to be looked for. As he liked to say, God is to be found
on the high street of life, in the busyness of our lives.
One of his favourite stories was that of the boy who
tossed a stone through a stained-glass window of the
Incarnation, nicking out the letter 'e' in the word
'Highest'. Instead of 'Glory to God in the Highest', the
inscription now read 'Glory to God in the High St'.
That, said MacLeod, is how it should have been left, or
perhaps with a swivelling panel for the letter 'e' so that
it could say both.

It was in the busy streets of Glasgow, then, that

MacLeod worked out, on the run, a spirituality both
mystical and political, looking more and more to the
spirituality of the early Celtic Church. In 1938 he made
the decision to begin to rebuild the ancient Abbey on
Iona, where in the sixth century St Columba had based
his Celtic mission. In part the work symbolized the
need to rebuild or rediscover the spirituality that Iona
represented for him. Thus began the present-day Iona
Community, which initially consisted of MacLeod,
young ministers in training and unemployed craftsmen.
They were committed not only to the restoration of the
monastic buildings on the island but to rediscovering a
discipline of prayer and rebuilding justice in their lives
and in the cities. With the Western world on the verge
of war, MacLeod and the young community also made
a commitment to re-establish the foundations for peace.

A prayer of MacLeod's during the rebuilding of the
Abbey on Iona draws on the themes of the community:

> It is not just the interior of these walls,
> it is our own inner beings you have renewed.
> We are your temple not made with hands.
> We are your body.
> If every wall should crumble,
> and every church decay, we are your habitation.
> Nearer are you than breathing,
> closer than hands and feet.
> Ours are the eyes with which you, in the mystery,
> look out in compassion on the world.
> So we bless you for this place,
> for your directing of us,
> your redeeming of us, and your indwelling.
> Take us 'outside the camp', Lord,

outside holiness,
out to where soldiers gamble, and thieves curse,
and nations clash at the cross-roads of the world. . . .
So shall this building continue to be justified.[9]

During these years MacLeod became an increasingly
controversial as well as prominent figure in the Church,
both internationally and within Scotland. The BBC
prevented him from broadcasting during the Second
World War because of his pacifism, but, both before and
after, MacLeod was a popular radio preacher throughout the British Empire. He was not beyond scheming
to reinforce his image as a preacher in the Columban
mould. The Celtic saints' love of nature and the animal
world was well known, and people often wondered
why the sea-gulls would call out just as MacLeod
began to broadcast his sermon on the radio. The simple
reason was that he had given instructions for fish to be
scattered around the Abbey as soon as he entered the
pulpit.

Although there were times of resistance to MacLeod,
and criticism of him from certain quarters never
ceased, in 1957 this Celtic visionary had so integrated
his spirituality with his churchmanship and gained such
respect throughout the Church that he was elected
Moderator of the General Assembly of the Church of
Scotland. Maybe even more astonishingly, about ten
years later he was appointed to the House of Lords.
MacLeod was now the Very Revd Lord MacLeod of
Fuinary. In the years to come further recognition from
Church and society followed, including the Templeton
International Prize for progress in religion. These
honours, he said, all confirmed that 'I never was a real
prophet.'

By the time MacLeod was in his nineties, many, especially among the younger generations, revered him as something of a saint. In 1988, when he visited the newly built MacLeod Centre for International Reconciliation on Iona, MacLeod entered the community room, stood still and began to recite the Lord's Prayer. Those with him, seeing the great man praying in the centre named after him, bowed their heads respectfully, but after the second phrase, MacLeod stopped, looked around him and said, 'I was only testing the acoustics!' Even to the end, he did not want his spirituality to be regarded as a pious practice separating him from life and from others, but rather as a search for God in the whole of life, in everything he said and did.

Who was this man? Was he just an exceptional visionary, or can he be seen to stand in the long tradition of Celtic spirituality that stretches back to Pelagius in the fourth century and includes a medieval mystic like John Scotus Eriugena and the centuries-old prayers of the people of the Western Isles? Celtic spirituality can be described as a way of seeing. What MacLeod shared with the stream of spirituality that had appeared early in British Christianity, was rejected by the Church at large and then resurfaced again and again in the Celtic world over the centuries, was its way of seeing or listening for God within the whole of life. One of MacLeod's best-known prayers was modelled on the ancient 'Breastplate' hymn of St Patrick, in which Christ is seen in all things:

Christ above us, Christ beneath us,
Christ beside us, Christ within us.
Invisible we see you, Christ above us,
With earthly eyes we see above us,
clouds or sunshine, grey or bright.

84

But with the eye of faith
we know you reign,
instinct in the sun ray,
speaking in the storm,
warming and moving all creation,
Christ above us. . . .

Invisible we see you, Christ beneath us.
With earthly eyes we see beneath us
stones and dust and dross. . . .
But with the eyes of faith,
we know you uphold.
In you all things consist and hang together.
The very atom is light energy,
the grass is vibrant,
the rocks pulsate.
All is in flux;
turn but a stone and an angel moves.
Underneath are the everlasting arms.
Unknowable we know you, Christ beneath us.

Inapprehensible we know you, Christ beside us.
With earthly eyes we see men and women,
exuberant or dull, tall or small.
But with the eye of faith,
we know you dwell in each.
You are imprisoned in the . . . dope fiend and the
    drunk,
dark in the dungeon, but you are there.
You are released, resplendent,
in the loving mother, . . . the passionate bride,
and in every sacrificial soul.
Inapprehensible we know you, Christ beside us.

Intangible, we touch you, Christ within us.
With earthly eyes we see ourselves,

dust of the dust, earth of the earth. . . .
But with the eye of faith,
we know ourselves all girt about of eternal stuff,
our minds capable of Divinity,
our bodies groaning, waiting for the revealing,
our souls redeemed, renewed.
Intangible we touch you, Christ within us.

Christ above us, beneath us,
beside us, within us,
what need have we for temples made with hands?[10]

The major characteristics of Celtic spirituality can be
found in MacLeod's mysticism. The first was his conviction of the essential goodness of creation and of the
image of God in humanity. Although MacLeod's greatness was that he held together the two ways of seeing
that were largely divided after Whitby, on this issue
of the essential goodness of creation he stood much
closer to Pelagius, for instance, than to Augustine, and
infinitely closer to the spirituality of the people of the
Western Isles than to the extreme Calvinism of the
Scottish Church that considered humanity to be totally
depraved. MacLeod saw creation as 'resplendent'. He
described the air of the eternal as 'seeping through the
physical'. The material realm of creation, he believed, is
shot through with spirit. 'What a wonderful world it is,'
he said, 'provided you believe in another world. Not
over against this world, but interlaced with it.'[11]

The imagery that comes across again and again in
MacLeod's writings is that of the everlasting pattern in
Celtic art, the threads of heaven and the threads of earth
inseparably interwoven. Christ is alive in both the material world and the spiritual. 'Christ, declares the Gospel,
is not just the Light of the Church, or just the life of

the converted soul. He is both because he is the Light and the Life of the *world*.'[12] And so in Christ everything is to be seen as 'every blessed thing'. All life at its heart is vibrant with God's life. In his prayers MacLeod would often refer, as prayers in the Celtic tradition had done before him, to God as the Life within all life. The following lines are taken from 'The Glory in the Grey':

Almighty God . . .
Sun behind all suns,
Soul behind all souls, . . .
show to us in everything we touch
and in everyone we meet
the continued assurance of thy presence round us,
lest ever we should think thee absent.
In all created things thou art there.
In every friend we have
the sunshine of thy presence is shown forth.
In every enemy that seems to cross our path,
thou art there within the cloud to challenge us to
    love.
Show to us the glory in the grey.
Awake for us thy presence in the very storm
till all our joys are seen as thee
and all our trivial tasks emerge as priestly
    sacraments
in the universal temple of thy love.[13]

The second characteristic of Celtic spirituality MacLeod shared is the belief that, although creation is essentially good and humanity at its deepest level still bears within itself the image of God, the world and each one of us is also streaked through with terrible darknesses. In *The Whole Earth Shall Cry Glory*, therefore, MacLeod tells us that, in the garden of the earth, as it were, and 'in the garden that is each of us, always the thorn'.

The thorn within us all that MacLeod was particularly aware of, and against which he preached passionately, was the thorn of violence. He taught that non-violence of the heart as well as non-violence of action are central to the gospel. Year after year, in the face of tremendous opposition, MacLeod would call upon the General Assembly of the Church of Scotland to take a firm stand on the issue of unilateral nuclear disarmament for Britain. The Assembly became so accustomed to voting against MacLeod that someone once suggested that if he were to speak in favour of nuclear arms the National Church would immediately vote for disarmament. In fact, in the end, MacLeod's campaign was successful. In one of his best-remembered articles on non-violence, MacLeod made his point with the Christ-mysticism that characterized his thinking:

Suppose the material order, as we have argued, is indeed the garment of Christ, the Temple of the Holy Ghost. Suppose the bread and wine, symbols of creation, are indeed capable of redemption awaiting its Christification. Then what is the atom but the emergent body of Christ? . . .

The Feast of the Transfiguration is August 6th. That is the day when we 'happened' to drop the bomb at Hiroshima. We took His body and we took His blood and we enacted a cosmic Golgotha. We took the key to love and we used it for bloody hell.

Nobody noticed. I am not being cheap about other people. I did not notice it myself. I was celebrating the Feast of the Transfiguration, in a gown and a cassock, a hood, a stole, white hands, saying with the whole Christian ministry, 'This is my body. This is my blood.'

The while our 'Christian civilization', without Church protest, made its assertion of the complete divorce between spirit and matter.

One man noticed. When the word came through to Washington of the dropping of the atom bomb – 'Mission successfully accomplished' – Dr Oppenheimer, in large degree in our name its architect, was heard to say, 'Today the world has seen sin.'[14]

MacLeod, like the stream of Celtic spirituality before him, saw creation as vibrant with God's life, and he saw also that it was bound, held down, by forces of darkness and yearning, as St Paul had seen, for redemption, for release. Salvation, therefore, meant being liberated from the evils that dominate us, in order that our essential goodness, and the original blessing of the earth, might be set free.

The third characteristic of MacLeod's Celtic spirituality, or way of seeing, was his sense of the immediacy of the spiritual realm, of God's presence in the whole of life. It included a keen mystical awareness of those who have gone before and of the host of heaven present among us on earth. Iona he often described as 'a thin place', in which the spiritual world is very close to the material. He was not speaking only of Iona, of course; for him the island was a symbol of the whole earth. For him, as for Alexander Scott and others in the Celtic tradition, the ladder that connects heaven and earth is everywhere present.

MacLeod admitted that the Abbey on Iona could

seem an easy place in which to believe in the living communion of saints. Yet sometimes, he said, it seemed 'to need all its granite strength to hold it to the ground against the battery and assault of demons'. Along with the sense that the life of heaven is interwoven with the things of the earth, MacLeod, too, clearly perceived the presence of evil.

The twentieth century, MacLeod believed, has been fearful of the invisible realm, of both its heights and its depths, the angelic and the demonic, and has tended to settle for a superficial materialism. The modern Church has tried to place a seal on the doors of hell, he said, only to hear the gates of heaven clang shut. The result has been what he called 'a demonic secularism':

> God grant that it will be given us to see the return of Michael; or, if not to us, to our children; or, if not to them. to our children's children, to see the return of Michael, . . . not to temples made with hands, but to this emergent universal temple of earth and sky and sea. . . . Angels must become our consciousness again, not floppy damsels in their nighties, but dynamic forces in their serried ranks 'the whole company of heaven'. . . . By all means let us say that the secular is the realm of God's activity and that He is in and through all things. But realize He has both let loose Satan there, for our disciplining, and that Christ is also there for our salvation.[15]

MacLeod's plea was for a recovery of the vision that would free us, individually and collectively, to see both the heights and the depths of the mystery in which we live, the glory within us and in the matter of creation as well as the darkness which, close and imprisoning, threatens each life.

In George MacLeod the stream of Celtic spirituality found new expression; most significantly, it was an expression that came from the very heart of the established Church. Among MacLeod's finest qualities was his unswerving loyalty to that Church, although he could not resist leavening it with the humour that for him always put things in perspective. Even his recollections of personally important moments in relation to the Church were not spared his humorous touch, as this account shows:

> The greatest honour of my life was being made Moderator of the General Assembly of the Church of Scotland. I wore my great-grandfather's moderatorial lace ruffles, and my great-uncle's moderatorial silver buckles, and I put my grandfather's rug on the moderatorial chair. . . . And there I stood before the Assembly looking like a medieval pirate.

The National Church had often misunderstood him and pulled in the opposite direction, but MacLeod consistently lived and prayed commitment to the Church. This prayer is entitled 'A Chaos of Uncalculating Love':

> It was your custom,
> to go to the temple,
> to the noisome temple
> sometime to the scandalised temple
> listening to the mumbo jumbo,
> but it was your custom to go.
> . . .

Give us grace in our changing day
to stand by the temple that is the present church,
the noisome temple
the sometime scandalised temple that is the present
    church,
listening sometime to what again seems mumbo
    jumbo.
Make it our custom to go
till the new outline of your Body for our day
becomes visible in our midst.[16]

MacLeod's vision and his passionate search for the outline of Christ's Body in the world continued well into
his nineties. With energy and enthusiasm, he continued
to discuss with the people who visited him in his last
years the vibrancy of matter and the urgent need for
non-violence. 'Blessed are the peace-makers,' he would
tell them, and then go on to say, for example, 'Sometimes I think I'll live to be a hundred – at least I think
so until lunch-time. In the afternoon I'm not so sure.'

In the summer of 1991, at the age of 96, MacLeod
died. The islanders of Iona seemed to know that when
he died the Abbey bell would toll, so that when a new
bell-ringer was being broken in, people would sometimes phone up and ask if Lord MacLeod had passed
away. When news of his death did come the bell was
tolled and islanders, visitors and the Abbey community
filled the Cathedral to remember him in silence and to
listen together to some of his prayers. 'A Veil Thin As
Gossamer' was the final prayer of George MacLeod's to
be read at that informal gathering at the Abbey on the
day he died:

Be thou, triune God, in the midst of us as we give
thanks for those who have gone from the sight of

earthly eyes. They, in thy nearer presence, still worship with us in the mystery of the one family in
heaven and on earth. . . .

If it be thy holy will, tell them how much we
love them, and how we miss them, and how we
long for the day when we shall meet with them
again. . . .

Strengthen us to go on in loving service of *all*
thy children. Thus shall we have communion with
thee, and, in thee, with our beloved ones. Thus
shall we come to know within ourselves that there
is no death and that only a veil divides, thin as
gossamer.[17]

Like the prayers of the Western Isles before him,
MacLeod's prayer had been written in the conviction
of the closeness of the saints, and that death is not a
departing from life but a returning to its Heart. In his
last year a young reporter asked him what he thought
about death. 'On the whole,' replied MacLeod, 'I'm in
favour of it.'

6 ✤ Two Ways of Listening: *John and Peter*

The stream of Celtic spirituality, from Pelagius in the fourth century to George MacLeod in the twentieth, is characterized by the expectation of finding God within, of hearing the living voice of God speaking from the very heart of life, within creation and within ourselves. It is a spirituality that recognizes the authority of St John and reflects his way of looking and listening for God. At the decisive Synod of Whitby in 664, where two distinct ways of seeing, represented by the Celtic and Roman missions, came into conflict, the former allied itself to John. Coleman of Lindisfarne argued that the Celtic tradition originated from St John, the disciple who was, he said, 'especially loved by our Lord'. Wilfrid, on the other hand, argued for the Roman mission, which, he claimed, was based on the authority of St Peter, whom he called 'the most blessed Prince of the Apostles'. The tragic outcome of the synod was not that it chose the Roman mission but that it neither made room within the Church for both ways of seeing or declared that both were firmly rooted in the gospel tradition.

The practice of listening for God within the whole of life was based on the perspective of St John's Gospel;

it is therefore not limited to the Celtic tradition, but found in various mystical traditions in the history of the Church. Celtic spirituality is, however, unique in the way in which it developed and cherished John's vision. It is important always to remember that Christianity is not confined to a single perspective; rather, it comprises a rich interweaving of approaches to God. It is not a ✓ question of choosing between the John and Peter traditions, but of attempting to hold them together. We need to ask how we can celebrate both and merge them into a spirituality for ourselves and the Church today.

The great Celtic theologian of the ninth century, John Scotus Eriugena, although sharing the mystical tradition of St John and its listening for God in all things, understood the need to make room for both John and Peter. The former, he believed, represents the way of contemplation, the latter, faithful action. Both disciples ran to the empty tomb of Jesus and both witnessed his resurrection. In a sense, they can be regarded as the male equivalents of Mary and Martha and as symbols of the tension between the contemplative and the active. This tension has always existed in the Church and we experience it ourselves in trying to find a balance between the inner and the outer. In this intensely materialistic and busy age, which sets great store by outward appearance and possessions and by activity, what is the balance that we need to recover in our spirituality, if we are to integrate the inner and the outer, and to allow the spiritual to shape our lives? If both the way of John and the way of Peter are to have a place in our spirituality, what are their distinct strengths and weaknesses?

In the New Testament the John tradition is of course best reflected by the Gospel according to St John. The Peter tradition, on the other hand, finds its clearest expression in the Gospel according to St Matthew, which includes the reference to Peter as the rock on which Christ will build his Church. By comparing these Gospels we can understand the conflict of Whitby and its aftermath and the tensions and complementarities between these two ways of seeing.

John's Gospel begins with the Word that was in the beginning: 'All things came into being through him, and without him not one thing came into being' (John 1:3). The perspective is a universal one. Matthew's Gospel, on the other hand, begins with the words, 'The book of the genealogy of Jesus Christ, the son of David, the son of Abraham' (Matthew 1:1). Here the perspective is particular. The tendency in the John tradition is always to see God in relation to the whole of creation, in relation to 'all things'. It refers, for instance, to the Light 'that enlightens every person coming into the world' (John 1:9). John's canvas is the whole cosmos. Like his symbol, the eagle in flight, he sees as from a height the whole of life, its beginning and its end. His perspective is infinite. In looking at one thing, the life of Christ, his vision includes all things, for Christ is the life of all life. The tendency in the Peter tradition, however, is to see God in relation to a particular people. In Matthew's Gospel God brings salvation to the world through a specific line of descent. Thus the first chapter reads like the record of a family tree. The symbol associated with his Gospel is that of a man on earth, so Matthew describes what is immediately in his line of vision, the details of a particular family and heritage. In writing about Jesus, he paints a vivid picture of a human family, its history and prophetic tradition.

The strength of the John tradition is that it produces

96

a spirituality that sees God in the whole of life and regards all things as inter-related. In all creation, and in all the people of creation, the light of God is there to be glimpsed, in the rising of the morning sun, in the moon at night and at the heart of the life of any person, even if that person is of an entirely different religious tradition or of no religious tradition. John's way of seeing makes room for an open encounter with the Light of life wherever it is to be found. As the history of Celtic spirituality shows, it is a tradition that can stand free of the four walls of the Church, for the sanctuary of God is not separate from but contained within the whole of creation. The strength of the Peter tradition is precisely that it does have four walls, as it were. It enshrines the light of truth within the Church and its traditions and sacraments. It is a rock, a place of security and shelter, especially in the midst of stormy change. It allows us, even in our times of personal confusion, to turn with faith to the familiar house of prayer where our mothers and fathers and those before them have for centuries found truth and guidance.

These ways of seeing can combine to create a spirituality that is simultaneously well-rooted in a specific tradition and open to God in the whole of life. Together they can provide access to the ancient treasury of the house of faith, while at the same time equipping us to discern God's presence in all life. If they are not held together, however, the result will be a spirituality in part cut off from the world and, in its religious constraints, separated from life, from the earth and its people. It may fear creation as an essentially threatening (to be tamed) and even godless place, doubting those of other faiths, or imagine that the Church's buildings and tradition contain the holy rather than simply symbolizing the holiness that is everywhere present. Alternatively, the division might produce a spirituality that, in an attempt to broaden its vision, is no longer connected to any Church and becomes cut off from the truths and mysteries traditionally protected by the walls of the Church. While retaining a strong sense of the inter-relatedness of all people and of the whole of creation, it may cease to learn from the great corpus of the Church's wisdom and become an individualistic spiri-tuality. The two traditions have often been pulled apart, but they are much stronger together. The truth of 'God with us' that is celebrated by particular people in par-ticular places need not be an exclusive celebration; it applies to every person and every form of life, because God is with and in all that has life.

The creative tension between these two ways of seeing is symbolized on Iona. Outside the main entrance to St Mary's Cathedral, on the island, stand the great Celtic crosses of St John and St Martin. There need be no discontinuity in worshipping at the foot of these crosses and then moving inside to continue worship within the stone walls of the Benedictine Abbey. Rather, the one experience can enrich the other. Being part of the song of creation and, as members of the Church, of the living communion of saints, are two aspects of the one mystery. Teilhard de Chardin, who was a scien-tist, a priest and one of the twentieth century's great Christian mystics, saw, for instance, that when the priest raises his hands in consecration over the bread and wine at the churches altar he is declaring all matter, all life, to be Christ's body and blood.

Most of us will have had the experience of walking to Church in the light of the morning or evening and feeling reluctant to leave the freshness of the wind or the colours of the sky to enter an enclosed building, sometimes terribly stifling or cluttered and unimaginative in design. Sometimes we need not the busyness of a church but the solitude of a hill to be still and attentive to God. On the other hand, most of us have also experienced in the words, silence and sacraments of Church liturgy an opening of our inner vision, so that on our return home we see the elements of creation around us with fresh eyes. And at times we can feel isolated in creation. As Coleridge wrote:

Alone on a wide wide sea:
So lonely 'twas, that God himself
Scarce seemed there to be.[1]

In times of trouble and loneliness, have we not all drawn comfort from singing hymns and saying prayers in a congregation of men and women who, like us, have known temptation, loss and emptiness?

Occasionally it is not the open air or the church that we desire, but both. My memory of an evening on the Isle of Wight is, I am sure, a universal sort of memory. Towards sunset, I was out walking, with open fields on one side and trees lining the path. The air was clear and calm and I was hearing the birds' closing song for the day. For a long time I stood under a great pine, looking at its height and feeling its ancient life, aware that all was being enfolded by the sun's last light. I did not have to move; I was alone. I could have had another ten minutes, but I chose to move and a minute later was standing in the chapel of Quarr Abbey listening to the monks chanting and allowing my prayers to rise with the incense. I knew that in two different ways I had experienced one continuous act of worship.

This does not mean that it is only in the beautiful,

in the glorious rays of the sunset and the fine singing of Benedictine monks, that the connection can be made between the bounded walls of a church sanctuary and the life around it. Equally, in times of confusion, betrayal or failure, when from our depths we are calling out for help, we often find that the words of a church service give voice to our yearnings. We may even discover that traditional prayers more truly express our despair than we can ourselves. Similarly, the Church can guide our longings for justice in the world. The words of the Old Testament prophetic tradition, for instance, will sometimes sharpen our sense of urgency and passion for justice in society.

An aspect of life that the Church has often found difficult to express is the passion for life that is within us and the delight in life's sensuousness. Certain traditions have wonderfully developed the use of the senses in worship. To experience the divine liturgy in Eastern Orthodoxy, for example, is to know a full religious incorporation of the senses, through light and colour, touch, sound and scent, but Western religious traditions have tended to stop short in approaching sensuality, especially where it relates to relationship and sexuality. The way in which the Church has so often either ignored or allegorized the Song of Songs and its clear delight in the goodness and God-givenness of sexual attraction and intimacy typifies religious inhibition, with its fear of passion and the sensual.

Early in Augustine of Canterbury's Roman mission to Britain at the end of the sixth century, there were signs of this fear and of a determination to enforce clerical celibacy. In a series of questions addressed to the Pope, Augustine had expressed concern about common practices he had discovered in the British Church. For instance, women took Communion while they were menstruating, as did men who had recently had sexual intercourse with their wives. 'These uncouth English people,' wrote Augustine, 'require guidance on all these matters.'[2] In response, Pope Gregory indicated that although it was not forbidden for women to receive Communion during menstruation it was 'commendable' for them to refrain from doing so during their period of 'defilement', as he called it. Also, a man who had 'approached' his wife should not enter a church before washing and should even wait until his 'heated desires cool in the mind'. The Pope added that, although the physical union of married people was not sinful, husbands and wives should have intercourse only in order to procreate and never 'for mere pleasure'.

The Gospels of John and Matthew reflect different perspectives in relation to pleasure and the senses. Their accounts of the woman who anointed Jesus with oil, for example, describe what was probably the same event in very different ways. In John's Gospel, the woman, Mary, takes a pound of costly perfume, anoints Jesus' feet and wipes them with her hair. 'The house,' says John, 'was filled with the fragrance of the perfume' (John 12:3). In Matthew's version, on the other hand, an unnamed woman is described simply as coming to Jesus and pouring oil on his head as he sits at table (Matthew 26:7). The fragrance of the perfume and the intimacy of the anointing and drying of Jesus' feet are entirely absent from this account. In John's Gospel there is a readiness to delight in the sensory and in the closeness of affection. Matthew is more cautious. John's spirituality accentuates the Light that is within all life, revealing a passion for life in its fullness. The body is regarded as good and intimacy becomes an expression of God's love. In the spirituality of the Peter tradition there is an awareness of the dangers of delighting in the senses. In time this awareness led to the extreme belief, shared by both Augustine of Hippo and his namesake in Canterbury, that sexual love is merely concupiscence.

In the modern age, with its obsession with the sexual, it is important to allow John's vision to help shape our spirituality. 'I have come that you may have life,' says Jesus in St John's Gospel, 'and that you may have it in abundance' (John 10:10). We need to regain confidence in the goodness of creation and thus of the body and of our sexuality, whether we are celibate, single or committed in relationship. This entails recovering a sense of the goodness of the creativity that is fundamental to creation's fruitfulness and continuity. We will not be able to address the perversity of our generation's fascination with sex by denying the essential goodness of our sexuality, but rather by declaring that it is deeply sacred, an essential part of who we are, and therefore reflecting the goodness of God's image in us. The John tradition encourages us to honour and delight in our sexual identity. This is where the two perspectives need to be held together. The John tradition encourages us to acknowledge the goodness of our physicalness and to understand that the sensual has a place in spirituality and can express God's love and creativity. The Peter tradition, on the other hand, can set boundaries to help us answer questions like, With whom should we be intimate? and, How does the goodness of the sensual relate to commitment in relationship, or to the demands of community life and society's well-being? Yes, let us passionately and uninhibitedly taste the goodness and delightfulness of creation, but let us also be alert to the laws that protect sustainability and wholeness in our relationships.

Another tension between the two ways of seeing is created by their distinct approaches to wrongdoing. How should we view our failures in relationship, for instance? John's Gospel includes the story of the woman taken in adultery (a story that today raises questions about its failure to mention the man who was guilty of adultery). Jesus tells those who want to stone the woman, 'Let anyone among you who is without sin be the first to throw a stone at her.' When no one condemns her, Jesus says, 'Neither do I condemn you. Go your way, and from now on do not sin again' (John 8:7–11). In Matthew's Gospel, on the other hand, we find these words: 'I say to you that every one who looks at a woman with lust has already committed adultery with her in his heart. If your right eye causes you to sin, tear it out and throw it away' (Matthew 5:28–30). John's tradition, espoused by Pelagius and others in the Celtic tradition, recognizes our capacity for goodness; even when we fail we are seen as essentially good, as capable of not failing. Christ is portrayed as forgiving and 'full of grace'. God's goodness is at the heart of the human and humanity is graced with the profound desire to be holy, as God is holy. In repenting of sin we are not turning away in order to be someone else, but re-turning to our true selves, made in the loveliness and goodness of the image of God.

The Peter tradition, on the other hand, underlines our capacity for sin and warns us to be on our guard against this tendency in ourselves and others. It sees Christ as the fulfilment of the Law, a corrective to our sinfulness. It approaches our behaviour with a caution that may be as wise as a serpent's, but can overlook the intrinsic good at the heart of each life. With Augustine this way of seeing led to the extreme conviction that the essential goodness in humanity was totally erased with Adam's fall.

In this area, perhaps above all others, we must recover a balance in our spirituality, believing and hoping in our God-given goodness on the one hand and being wise and alert to sinful leanings on the other. Is it not always necessary to pursue two approaches to our failings, the transformative and the surgical? We should be able to cut out deep-seated wrongs and provide at the same time the right conditions for goodness to flourish. Is this not how the body operates? The aim of medicine, therapy, rest and surgery is always to enable the healthy energy deep within us to assert itself against any disease or malaise that is threatening our essential well-being. In the same way, are we not to be liberating the image of God that is within us? If we do not, how will we deal with ourselves and others in the midst of terrible failure? How, for instance, will we deal with a young teenager who helped kick to death a young man because he was homosexual? Are we to say that she is evil at the core of her being and should be locked away for the rest of her life, unless she can become something totally other than what she is? The conviction of Celtic spirituality is that her evil behaviour sprang not from the very heart of her life but from a deep confusion and loss; if she is given the grace to recover some of the goodness that was hers in infancy she will gradually be transformed into her true self. In the process, of course, she will need to be protected from her tendency to evil. However, punishment and watchfulness cannot in themselves restore people's goodness; this can be done only by releasing their true essence, made in the image of God.

In the John tradition transformation occurs through love. 'I give you a new commandment,' says Jesus, 'that you love one another. Just as I have loved you, you also should love one another' (John 13:34). Change will come through love. John's spirituality is guided above all else by a sense of the welling up of love from life's deepest springs, the place of God's abiding. In the Peter tradition, on the other hand, great confidence is placed in the outward strength and rightness of the law handed down by religious tradition. Following God's law will bring about change for the good in our lives, both individually and collectively. 'Do not think that I have come to abolish the law or the prophets,' says Jesus in Matthew's Gospel, 'I have come not to abolish but to fulfil. For truly I tell you, until heaven and earth pass away, not one letter, not one stroke of a letter, will pass from the law until all is accomplished' (Matthew 5:18). Part of this tradition are social justice and charity, including the practices, set forth in Matthew 25, of feeding the hungry, clothing the poor, caring for the sick and attending to those in prison. The love of others is to be combined with the law of righteousness. Otherwise, at one extreme there may be a vague, unproductive enthusiasm for the sacredness of all life and, at the other, a joyless moral dutifulness. On its own, neither approach can bring about the profound changes that are needed in our lives and in the wider relationships of the world.

In the New Testament, not only are their different perspectives generally united, but John and Peter themselves often appear together. At the Last Supper, for example, they are next to one another and after

Jesus' arrest they are the two who follow him. Separated at the crucifixion, they later run together to Jesus' empty tomb. In the Acts of the Apostles they are referred to as sharing the experience of imprisonment. One of their greatest shared experiences, however, is the transfiguration, described in Matthew's Gospel. On the mountain they see Christ as the Light of God and are instructed to 'listen to him' (Matthew 17:5).

John and Peter did listen, in different ways, and this is why it is important to bring together their distinct perspectives and draw on the complementary Gospel traditions. The brief historical sketches in this book have shown how the Church has been weakened over the centuries by its rejection of Celtic spirituality and the latter's development of the mysticism of St John. The Church would have been infinitely richer if it had embraced both Pelagius and Augustine, affirming the essential goodness in every life while remaining alert to the evils that can destroy us. This would have provided surer foundations for integrating our spirituality with the whole of life and with what is most natural. At the Synod of Whitby, why could the way of John not have been held together with the way of Peter? The Celtic mission, which acknowledged the light present even in those who have not heard the gospel, complemented the Roman mission, with its emphatic claims of the uniqueness of the gospel. The two were not mutually exclusive. The Church was the poorer for forcing Celtic spirituality underground, so that for centuries it survived primarily on the Celtic fringes of Britain, among people unsupported in their spirituality by clergy. Would not the Church and the world have been better prepared to meet the challenges of the modern world – including ecological crises – if they had learned from Celtic spirituality instead of rejecting it? Would they not have been enriched by the awareness that God's light is within creation as well as transcending it? Why was the Church so frightened when, in the nineteenth century, men like Scott and MacDonald taught that we are a reflection of God's image, the divine being inextricably interwoven with the human? Would it not have been enlarged in its spirit by affirming that our creativity, sexuality and passion for life can be expressions of the life of God?

Finally, in the twentieth century, when the John tradition was reflected in George MacLeod and others, why did their conviction that God is the Light of the world (rather than just a religious aspect of it) not burst open the doors of the Church to the world? If it had more wholeheartedly accepted this belief, the Church would surely have avoided many of the dangers of irrelevance, which often characterize it today. Could it not have redefined its boundaries? Instead of being shut off behind its four walls, upholding a spirituality that too often looks away from life, could it not have transformed itself into a kind of side chapel for the world? Our churches might then have become places where we could more easily step into and out of daily life and be reminded that the real cathedral of God is the whole of creation. If the Church's symbols and rituals pointed more clearly to the world as God's dwelling-place, we might then more fully rediscover that God's heartbeat can be heard in the whole of life and at the heart of our own lives, if we will only listen.

Notes

Chapter 1 Listening for the Goodness: *Pelagius*

1. Robert Van de Weyer (ed.), *The Letters of Pelagius*, Arthur James, 1995, 58.
2. *The Letters of Pelagius* 36.
3. *The Letters of Pelagius* 71.
4. *The Letters of Pelagius* 72.
5. *The Letters of Pelagius* 48.
6. *The Letters of Pelagius* 46.
7. B. R. Rees (ed.), 'Letter to Demetrias', *Letters of Pelagius and His Followers*, Boydell, 1991, pp. 29–70, 2.2.
8. *The Letters of Pelagius* 66.
9. *The Letters of Pelagius* 59.
10. 'Letter to Demetrias' 8.1.
11. *The Letters of Pelagius* 55.
12. *The Letters of Pelagius* 62.
13. 'Letter to Demetrias' 3.3
14. 'Letter to Demetrias' 6.3.
15. 'Letter to Demetrias' 8.4.
16. *The Letters of Pelagius* 67.
17. *The Letters of Pelagius* 81.

Chapter 2 Listening within Creation: *Eriugena*

1. John Scotus Eriugena (trans. Christopher Bamford),

The Voice of the Eagle, Lindisfarne Press, 1990, Homily XI.

2. John Scotus Eriugena (trans. John O'Meara), *Periphyseon* (The Division of Nature), Bellarmin, 1987, 681D.
3. Eriugena, *The Voice of the Eagle*, Homily XVII.
4. Eriugena, *Periphyseon*, 896B.

Chapter 3 Listening for God in All Things: *Carmina Gadelica*

1. Alexander Carmichael (ed.), *Carmina Gadelica* III, Scottish Academic Press, 1976, p. 233.
2. *Carmina Gadelica* III, p. 215.
3. Alexander Carmichael (ed.), *Carmina Gadelica* I, Constable, 1900, p. 41.
4. *Carmina Gadelica* III, p. 93.
5. *Carmina Gadelica* III, p. 61.
6. *Carmina Gadelica* III, p. 287.
7. *Carmina Gadelica* III, p. 307.
8. *Carmina Gadelica* III, p. 309.
9. *Carmina Gadelica* I, p. 3.
10. *Carmina Gadelica* III, p. 25.
11. *Carmina Gadelica* III, p. 363.
12. *Carmina Gadelica* III, p. 339.
13. *Carmina Gadelica* III, p. 367.
14. K. H. Jackson (trans.), *A Celtic Miscellany*, Penguin, 1971, p. 109.
15. *Carmina Gadelica* III, p. 53.
16. *Carmina Gadelica* III, p. 21.
17. *Carmina Gadelica* III, p. 207.
18. *Carmina Gadelica* III, p. 13.
19. *Carmina Gadelica* III, pp. 3, 7.
20. *Carmina Gadelica* III, p. 187.
21. *Carmina Gadelica* III, p. 321.
22. *Carmina Gadelica* I, p. xxiii.
23. *Carmina Gadelica* I, p. xxii.

24. *Carmina Gadelica* III, p. 351.
25. *Carmina Gadelica* III, p. 329.
26. *Carmina Gadelica* III, p. 383.

Chapter 4 Listening with the Imagination: *George MacDonald*

1. *The Westminster Confession of Faith*, ch. 6, sections 2, 4.
2. *See* J. Philip Newell, unpublished Ph.D. Thesis, *A. J. Scott and His Circle*, University of Edinburgh, 1981.
3. Alexander J. Scott, 'Lectures on the Harmony of Natural and Revealed Truth', *The Woolwich Gazette*, 12 September 1840.
4. Alexander J. Scott, *Suggestions on Female Education*, Maberly, 1849, p. 32.
5. Alexander J. Scott, *Two Discourses*, Darling, 1848, p. 36.
6. Alexander J. Scott, 'Social Systems of the Present Day', *The Woolwich Gazette*, 19 December 1840.
7. Alexander J. Scott, 'Introductory Discourse on Revelation', *Lectures on the Epistle to the Romans*, Darling, 1838, p. 4.
8. Scott, 'Introductory Discourse on Revelation', p. 7.
9. Scott, 'Introductory Discourse on Revelation', p. 4.
10. Scott, *Lectures on the Epistle to the Romans*, p. 27.
11. Alexander J. Scott, 'Social Systems of the Present Day', *The Woolwich Gazette*, 2 January 1841.

Chapter 5 Listening and Acting: *George MacLeod*

1. *See* Ronald Ferguson, *George MacLeod*, Collins, 1990.
2. Ronald Ferguson (ed.), *Daily Readings with George MacLeod*, Fount, 1991, p. 61.
3. *Daily Readings with George MacLeod*, p. 21.
4. *Daily Readings with George MacLeod*, p. 26.
5. *Daily Readings with George MacLeod*, p. 67.

6. *Daily Readings with George MacLeod*, pp. 36–7.
7. *Daily Readings with George MacLeod*, pp. 54–5.
8. *Daily Readings with George MacLeod*, p. 37.
9. George F. MacLeod (ed. Ronald Ferguson), *The Whole Earth Shall Cry Glory*, Wild Goose Publications, 1985, p. 45.
10. *The Whole Earth Shall Cry Glory*, p. 16.
11. *Daily Readings with George MacLeod*, p. 84.
12. *Daily Readings with George MacLeod*, p. 67.
13. *The Whole Earth Shall Cry Glory*, pp. 13–14.
14. *Daily Readings with George MacLeod*, pp. 68–9.
15. *Daily Readings with George MacLeod*, pp. 81–3.
16. *The Whole Earth Shall Cry Glory*, p. 39.
17. Adaptation of prayer from *The Whole Earth Shall Cry Glory*, p. 60.

Chapter 6 Two Ways of Listening: *John and Peter*

1. Samuel Taylor Coleridge, 'The Rime of the Ancient Mariner', Part VII, lines 598–600.
2. Bede, *Ecclesiastical History of the English People*, I.27.